IMAGES
of America

DOUGLAS

IMAGES
of America

DOUGLAS

Cindy Hayostek

ARCADIA
PUBLISHING

Published by Arcadia Publishing
Charleston SC, Chicago IL, Portsmouth NH, San Francisco CA

Library of Congress Catalog Card Number: 2008936540

For all general information contact Arcadia Publishing at:
Telephone 843-853-2070
Fax 843-853-0044
E-mail sales@arcadiapublishing.com
For customer service and orders:
Toll-Free 1-888-313-2665

Visit us on the Internet at www.arcadiapublishing.com

Dedicated with love to Cathy, Linda, and B. J., who always listen patiently to their mother's stories about Douglas and its residents.

CONTENTS

ACKNOWLEDGMENTS

This book took shape after I met Jared Jackson at an Arizona Historical Society convention. Immediately he believed Douglas deserved a book about its history; he's been a great editor. Photographs were generously provided by Roy Manley, Holly Berryhill, Armando Elías, Susan Krentz, Frank Roqueni, Bruce Whetten, City of Douglas, Douglas Cowbelles, Douglas Art Association, Douglas Elks Douglas Historical Society, and Cochise County Historical Society. Elizabeth Ames of the latter organization was always available to unlock museum doors and help in other ways. Connie Kazal, granddaughter of Alfred Paul, and her husband, Albert Kazal, critiqued the manuscript, as did Roy Manley. Two retired Douglas Reduction Works employees, superintendent Sam Sorich and master mechanic Frank Kenyon, checked the smelter chapter. All photographs are from the Cochise County Historical Society collection unless otherwise noted.

INTRODUCTION

As the year 1900 began, the southern end of the Sulphur Springs Valley was simply an amply watered area often used for cattle roundups. But changes were coming to the southeast corner of what was then known as the Arizona Territory. This was because the directors of Phelps Dodge and Company, a leading copper producer in the United States, had decided to build a new smelter outside the confines of the canyon that held its Copper Queen Mine and Bisbee, Arizona. Although the cattle roundup site was 25 miles east of Bisbee, it was all downhill—an attractive economy when considering heavily loaded railroad cars.

The roundup area was also downhill from Pilares de Nacozari, about 75 miles south in Sonora. In 1899, Phelps Dodge had, upon the recommendation of its consultant Dr. James Douglas, purchased a copper mine there.

In the autumn of 1900, crews began laying railroad tracks out of Bisbee, but few knew where the tracks were going. Doctor Douglas's eldest son, James S., and some associates did know however, and they formed the International Land and Improvement Company to survey and stake a town site. James S. was company president.

Almost by chance, a Bisbee butcher and merchant named Charles A. Overlock happened upon the staked International Land and Improvement Company land while he was on a cattle-buying trip to a ranch east of the Sulphur Springs Valley. When Overlock discovered the International Land and Improvement Company had failed to file its claim paperwork promptly, he immediately did so in the name of the Erie Townsite Company, which he formed with Alfred Paul, Lemuel Shattuck, and two other Bisbee friends.

Before 1900 was over, Overlock went to his town site and erected a frame building that became an office and headquarters for his lumberyard. The Erie Company started to fence its site, and the International Land and Improvement Company began subdividing its land. Fortunately good business sense prevailed and the International Land and Improvement Company took in the Erie men as partners.

In January 1901, an International Land and Improvement Company engineer, E. G. Howe, platted a town with wide streets and large, rectangular residential and business blocks. James S. Douglas suggested naming the new town after his father. In February 1901, the International Land and Improvement Company began selling lots priced at $25 to $250, and the boom was on. By 1905, some business lots commanded $10,000 price tags.

At first, the people who flocked to Douglas lived in a raggedy collection of tents and shacks around a hand-dug water well at Eleventh Street and H Avenue. But within a short time, the International Land and Improvement Company established a subsidiary, the Douglas Traction and Light Company, which provided electricity, an ice plant, telephones, and a streetcar system. Douglas is one of only five towns in Arizona that had a street railway.

Within two years, Douglas had 1,500 houses. Cultural amenities such as a library, school, and churches began appearing. Four churches, each a different Protestant denomination, eventually were built on the four corners of one block—a fact later publicized by *Ripley's Believe It or Not* newspaper columns. One of those churches, St. Stephens Episcopal, sponsored what may be the first Boy Scout troop in Arizona.

Late in 1902, the Calumet and Arizona Mining Company (C&A), another copper firm with Bisbee holdings, began operations at a smelter that it had rushed to build in Douglas. The Copper Queen smelter did not heat up until March 1904. By 1906, the Copper Queen was processing 3,500 tons of ore each day and the C&A 1,500 tons. Between them, the two smelters employed 1,000 men.

These workers required a variety of support services, including boardinghouses, laundries, banks, and theaters. Since the majority of the population was male, there were numerous barbershops, billiard halls, almost 40 saloons, a red-light district, and the Copper City Brewing Company—the largest brewery in Arizona before Prohibition.

Another sizeable Douglas employer was the El Paso and Southwestern Railroad section headquarters, which included a roundhouse, shops, and massive passenger depot. Douglas was the only city in Arizona with railroads leaving in all four directions: south to Nacozari, east to New Mexico and El Paso, north to Gleeson/Courtland and Willcox, and west to Bisbee and Tucson.

The railroads meant Douglas developed into a major shipping location for cattle from both sides of the border. Douglas also became a jumping-off point for those who prospected and started small mining operations in Mexico. In addition, Douglas was the center of much intrigue before the Mexican Revolution broke out in 1910.

Agua Prieta, the Sonoran city that developed across the border from Douglas, was the site of two revolutionary battles. The 1911 battle was one of the first in the Mexican Revolution. Commanders of the second battle in 1915 were Pancho Villa and Plutarco Elías Calles, a future president of Mexico.

Concern that the Mexican Revolution would overflow into Douglas led to the establishment of an army camp on the town's eastern edge. Called Camp Douglas in its early days, the installation became Camp Harry J. Jones in 1916 and contributed to the city's economy into the 1930s.

The largest military presence in Douglas during World War II was a U.S. Army Air Corps field north of town. It was a natural outgrowth of Douglas residents' ongoing fascination with aviation, which started in 1910 when half a dozen enthusiasts built and flew a glider that they turned into an airplane. Others established a municipal airport where many aviation firsts took place.

Other Douglas residents loved automobiles, and in 1920 they attended a ceremony dedicating the longest hard-surfaced road in Arizona. The Bisbee-Douglas Highway sparked development of tourism, which led to the country's first motel on Seventeenth Street.

Douglas also had more formal lodgings, including the Gadsden Hotel. Its architect was Henry Charles Trost, a nationally known professional who also oversaw a 1918 addition to Douglas's Young Men's Christian Association (YMCA) building—perhaps the first YMCA in Arizona.

The original Gadsden, erected in 1907 and named in a contest, burned down in 1928. Rebuilt by its owners, Franklin and Mary Mackey, the new Gadsden featured an impressive lobby, over 100 rooms, and full services that made it one of the premier hotels in the Southwest.

Another architect, Eugene Durfee, planned the Grand Theater. Opened in 1919, the Grand Theater lived up to its name. Celebrities such as Anna Pavlova, John Phillip Sousa, and Ginger Rogers appeared on its stage, as well as countless local performers in dance recitals, plays, and high school graduation ceremonies.

Ben Levy commissioned Durfee to build a home for him at 1100 Tenth Street. Levy was one of two brothers who founded a series of department stores bearing their name. Levy's was a Southwestern institution that today is part of the Macy's chain.

The Levys were members of Douglas's active Jewish community. From its earliest days, the town was multinational in its composition and outlook. There were many residents who originally hailed from Canada, others from the Balkan countries, still others from what is now Lebanon, and many from Mexico.

In addition to the celebrities appearing on the Grand Theater's stage, others played baseball in town. Hal Chase, Chick Gandil, and Buck Weaver, major league players banned from professional ball after the 1919 Black Sox scandal, played for the Douglas Blues, a semipro team in the unsanctioned Copper League in the mid-1920s.

The passion Douglas residents had for baseball was apparent during the 1950s too, when the Copper Kings, a major league farm team, set a record enshrined in the Baseball Hall of Fame in Cooperstown, New York, that is unlikely to ever be equaled.

The sports fervor Douglasites display also supports the Douglas High School football team's ongoing series with Bisbee. Begun in 1906, it is one of the oldest prep school rivalries in the country and definitely the oldest in the state. The winner of the yearly game keeps the Copper Pick trophy.

Ranchers and farmers from the area surrounding Douglas have always been an important part of the town's economy and spirit. They shipped their agricultural products from Douglas, and conducted other business there.

Perhaps the most famous of these people was John Slaughter, who had been a Cochise County sheriff late in the 1800s. His generously watered ranch, 15 miles east of Douglas, hosted hundreds of friends, family members, and guests. Today the ranch, after a careful restoration by the Johnson Historical Museum of the Southwest, is a popular destination for tourists and locals alike.

A major change occurred in Douglas during 1987 when the last smelter closed permanently. Mayor Ben F. Williams Jr., anticipating this event, saw to it that several state prison units were built so as to provide employment for displaced smelter workers. Today the Arizona prison system is a major employer in the area, along with other law enforcement agencies such as the U.S. Customs and Border Patrol.

Another component of the area economy is border trade. With roots in the 1960s, the twin plant (*maquiladora*) industry in Douglas–Agua Prieta has produced electronic parts used in space shuttles and microphones used in Burger King restaurants, as well as millions of seat belts and pieces of clothing.

The enthusiasm Mexican residents have for shopping in the United States resulted in the development of a new Douglas shopping area. Beginning in 1992 with construction of the largest Safeway in Arizona, the development now includes a Super Wal-Mart and a number of smaller firms in a district where, as of this writing, a Best Western hotel is under construction.

Also under way is the rehabilitation of an old Douglas building to accommodate Advanced Call Center Technologies, a firm whose purpose is implicit in its name. Advanced Call Center Technologies plans to have almost 700 Douglas employees by 2012.

Because of its history, Douglas was always more than just a smelter town. Today Douglas is more than just a border town, as it retains a vigor shown in its past that bodes well for its future.

One

EARLY YEARS

In February 1901, two events occurred with long-term effects on Douglas. The first was the railroad from Bisbee reached the town site and work began on tracks to Nacozari, Sonora. The second event was passage of a congressional bill establishing the Douglas Port of Entry.

About the same time, a business district began taking shape east of the railroad tracks, and people built houses around this commercial core. Utilities included electricity, manufactured gas, telephones, and a water and sewer system paid for by a bond passed in 1906.

The city incorporated in May 1905. Charles Overlock served as the first mayor until William Adamson became the first elected mayor. Overlock founded several businesses and built a splendid house at 757 Eighth Street. Adamson, after supervising Copper Queen smelter construction, bought the Arizona Gypsum Plaster Company, a firm whose block and plaster is evident in many buildings today.

By 1907, the area had over 11,000 inhabitants, including the suburb of Pirtleville, northwest of Douglas. During their free time, residents could enjoy bowling alleys, tennis courts, swimming pools, a country club, concerts by the city band in Tenth Street Park, or baseball games in Sportsmen's Park, a stadium east of San Antonio Avenue, between Eighth and Ninth Streets.

There were plenty of community activities, many sponsored by unique groups. The Thirteen Club, composed of 13 socially prominent bachelors, spoofed superstition at their dances. Another group, the Sociedad Mutualista de Obreros Mexicanos (Mexican Workers Mutual Aid Society), offered social activities and life insurance to its Hispanic membership.

The boomtown atmosphere disappeared during an economic recession following World War I, but by 1924 Douglas again prospered. That year, the El Paso and Southwestern Railroad merged with Southern Pacific Railroad.

In 1925, a media frenzy beset Douglas–Agua Prieta following the reappearance of famous evangelist Aimee Semple McPherson after she had vanished for six weeks.

With the rest of the country, Douglas struggled through the Great Depression. By the end of the 1930s however, Douglas again was posed to flourish.

The Douglas Traction and Light Company provided several utilities to Douglasites. In the above photograph, community leaders completed the town's first telephone call in 1902. On the left is James East, a lawman who captured Billy the Kid in 1880s New Mexico and became Douglas police chief in 1910. The white-haired man holding a receiver to his ear is Fletcher Doan, a retired Arizona Superior Court judge living in Douglas. The photograph below shows the Traction and Light Company's electricity and ice-generating plant, east of Railroad Avenue between Twelfth and Thirteenth Streets. Arizona Public Service operated the ice plant into the late 1950s, razed it in 1973, and now has a warehouse and maintenance yard on the site. (Below, courtesy Roy Manley.)

A patriotic community event drew Douglasites from Twelfth Street southward down G Avenue in this photograph taken about 1910. The large, two-piece building on the right is the first Gadsden Hotel. Other visible landmark businesses include Phelps Dodge Mercantile and First National Bank on the right and the Brophy Building and Arizona Drug Store on the left. (Courtesy Roy Manley.)

Delivery vehicles, motorized and horse-drawn, lined up south of Phelps Dodge Mercantile building, whose corner is on the right in this c. 1912 photograph. A second-story walkway connects the mercantile with its warehouse (center building). The space between the two allowed for easy unloading of merchandise out of railroad boxcars. The warehouse was torn down in 1956 to create a parking lot. The structure with the tall spire is city hall, whose open white doors suggest warm weather.

Many Douglas residents turned out for this 1907 drilling contest held at the intersection of Railroad Avenue and Tenth Street. The YMCA building, believed to be the first such in Arizona, was only a year old. YMCA programs were so popular that in 1918 its directors added an extension to the building's southern end. Several generations of Douglasites bowled in the "YM," swam in its pool, and played basketball on its court. A non-profit corporation today hopes to renovate the building, which lost its YMCA affiliation in the 1960s. (Courtesy Douglas Historical Society.)

Established in 1905 by Henry and William Reno, the Copper City Brewing Company was the largest brewery in Arizona before Prohibition. It also appears in the image at the top of the page; its smokestack is to the left of the power pole. When Arizona "went dry" in 1913, Copper City Brewing Company switched to bottling soft drinks as the People's Ice and Manufacturing Company. The building burned in 1918 and its equipment was sold to a Culiacan, Sinaloa, brewery a few years later.

The International Laundry Company had just moved into 433 Twelfth Street when these photographs were taken in 1914. The image above shows the building's exterior and delivery crew; in the photograph below, washing equipment is overflowing with suds. Douglas pioneer Charles A. Nichols ran the business from 1902 until 1940 when he sold it to the Huish family. They ran it as Nu-Way Laundry and Drycleaning until 1997, when the building burned down.

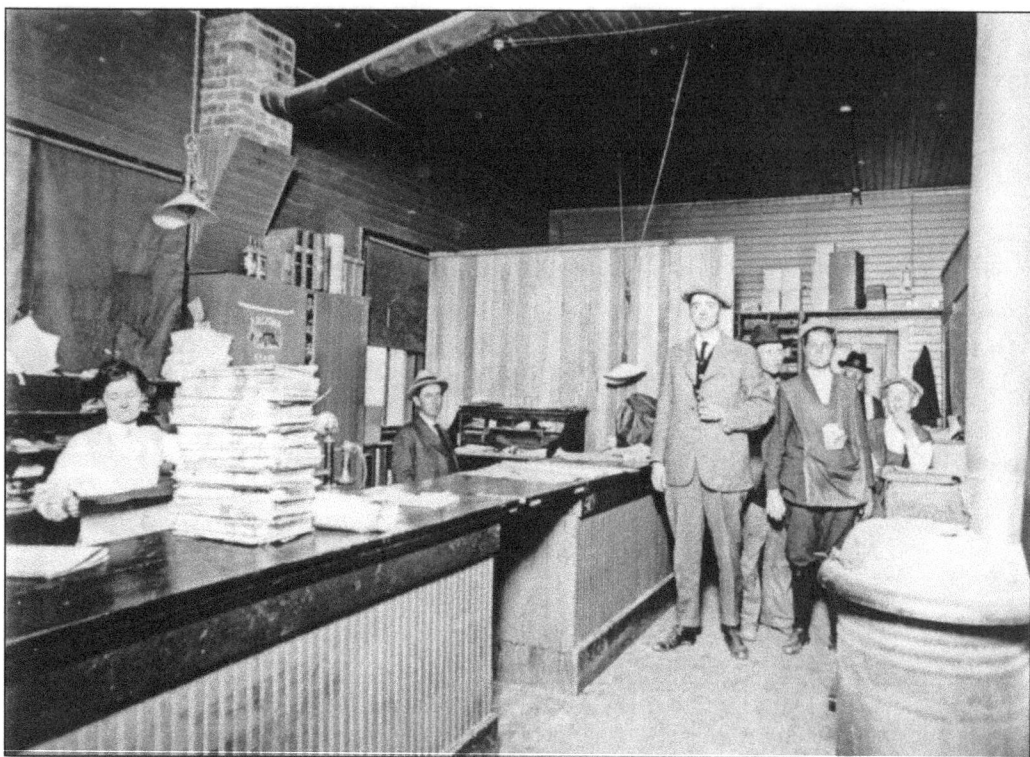

Four newspapers were published in 1912 in Douglas. *The International-American* (whose circulation office is the photograph above), at 537 Twelfth Street, was a daily that was Democratic in its politics. The *Daily Dispatch* (whose row of linotype machines is in the photograph below), at 530 Eleventh Street, was a daily that supported the Republican Party. The *Douglas Industrial* was printed weekly in Spanish. Little is known about the *Southwestern Mining Recorder*. The *International-American* and the *Daily Dispatch* merged in 1925, leaving Douglas with just the *Daily Dispatch*.

In 1907, Dr. F. W. Randall offered the Tonalene Liquor Cure in this building at 406 Eighth Street. The building became known as the Mexican Hospital since it was where Randall, standing on the balcony next to the Mexican flag, treated casualties from the 1911 Battle of Agua Prieta. Later the *Sociedad Mutualista de Obreros Mexicanos* (Mexican Workers Mutual Aid Society) bought the building for its headquarters.

Library Hall, in the 600 block, originally faced F Avenue and was a community center that hosted school classes, church services, dances, and other events. In 1916, to make room for a new post office, workers moved the building to the location shown, facing Tenth Street. By then it was the Copper Queen Library; today it is the Douglas Art Association's Little Gallery. Removal of the bell tower occurred about 1942.

In 1903, Douglasites approved a $20,000 bond that built the city's first school, a two-story brick edifice in the 700 block of Seventh Street, seen below. As the photograph above demonstrates, conditions were crowded. To relieve that, the school district built 10 schools in 10 years. This was part of a strong emphasis that Douglas residents consistently placed on education throughout the years.

This unique slide, built in the backyard of the O. O. Hammill house at 1122 Eleventh Street, was the invention of Bill Hammill (right). His sister Marion stands on the garage roof, while Bill Gibson and Charles Fleming shoot down the slide. O. O. Hammill founded Douglas Drug Store and then constructed his home, which was the first building east of A Avenue.

The Douglas Boy Scout Band posed for this photograph in 1928. It was taken in front of the Palomar Hotel at 433 Tenth Street with John Phillip Sousa (in the dark uniform), the "March King." Flanking Sousa are band director Bill Hanson (right) and band manager Lynn Palmer (left). The band was part of the Boy Scout movement in Douglas, which had perhaps the first troop in Arizona, founded in 1911 by O. O. Hammill. (Courtesy Douglas Historical Society.)

The Grand Theater, billed as the finest between San Antonio and Los Angeles, opened January 25, 1919. The Grand Theater's architect, Eugene Durfee, later designed the Fox Theater in Tucson for the Grand Theater's owners, the Diamos-Xalis family and their Lyric Amusement Company. Appearing on the Grand Theater stage were vaudeville acts and celebrities such as Ruth St. Denis, as well as local dance recitals and Douglas High School graduation ceremonies. The Grand Theater closed about 1958 and fell into disrepair, but today the Douglas Arts and Humanities Association is gradually restoring the building.

In 1919, more people lived in Douglas than today, yet the town site was half the size of today's city. So where did 18,000 people live? Many lived in boardinghouses such as this one, called the Leslie, at 637 Ninth Street, of which Mary Calisher was the proprietor. Most likely, she is the woman standing in the doorway. Ed Fortin, second from the right in the front row, was a typical boarder. He was a men's clothing salesman for Phelps Dodge Mercantile. (Courtesy Roy Manley).

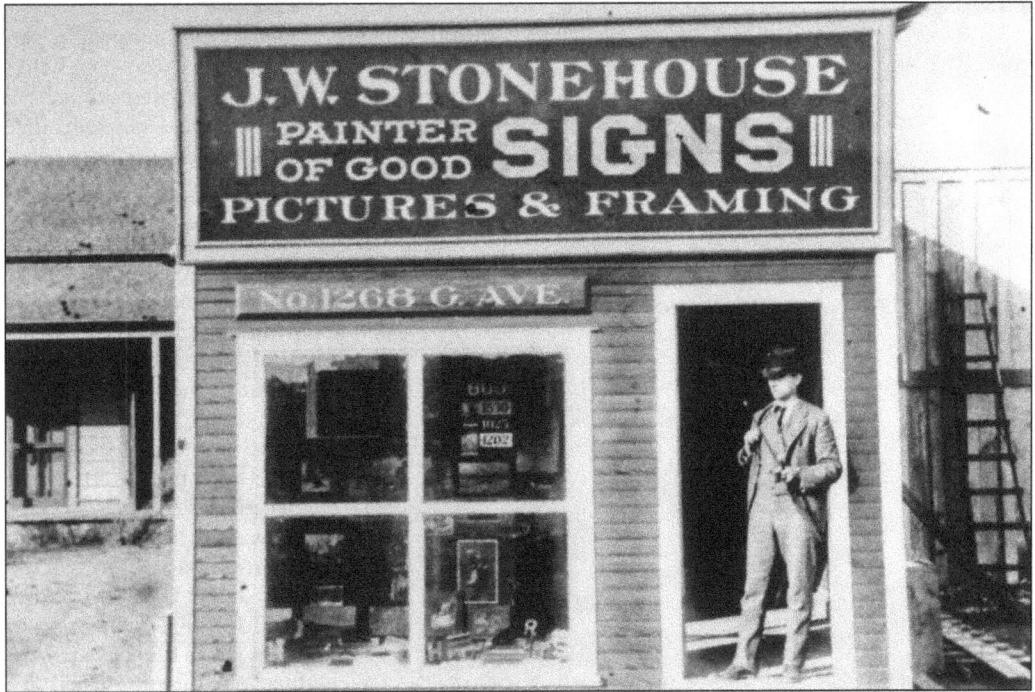

J. W. Stonehouse stands in the doorway of his G Avenue store in this 1908 photograph. Stonehouse painted many address signs for Douglas homes and businesses during the town's early years. Douglas streets begin with First Street next to the border and run numerically north. Douglas avenues west of Florida Avenue are alphabetical. Lot numbers incorporate block numbers with even numbers on the north side of streets and west side of avenues. Stonehouse went to Colorado in 1913 to establish a company that today is the largest manufacturer of industrial safety signs in the country.

In addition to being Douglas's first mayor, Charles A. Overlock (upper left) was the town's first postmaster and a member of an early school board. His Douglas Lumber Company office was the town's first building. He also dealt in real estate and had a grocery and feed store after serving as a U.S. Marshal in Arizona. William M. Adamson, (upper right) supervised Copper Queen smelter construction before acquiring what became Arizona Gypsum Plaster Company. He put his engineering skills to use as a director of the Douglas Traction and Light Company before becoming the first elected mayor. Robert B. Sims (left) was an accountant and city councilman when elected to be a delegate at Arizona's Constitutional Convention in 1910. That led to his appointment as the first state director of prisons, where he instituted a prisoner work program still used today. (The two above, courtesy City of Douglas; at left, Douglas Elks.)

Alfred C. Lockwood (upper left) was an attorney in Douglas when he married the town's first schoolteacher, Daisy Lincoln. He became an Arizona Supreme Court judge, and the couple's oldest child, Lorena, became Arizona's first female Supreme Court justice. William H. Brophy (upper right) was general manager of Phelps Dodge Mercantile Company and Bank of Bisbee president. He drowned in 1922, and his will provided for establishment of Brophy High School in Phoenix. In 1924, his widow established Loretto School in Douglas to memorialize him and a daughter who died young. B. A. Packard (right) was a cattleman, merchant, and territorial senator before moving to Douglas. His First National Bank, at 940 G Avenue, had international influence as did the man himself. (All author's collection.)

On June 15, 1914, Douglas businessman Matt Barasic opened the Natatorium at 660 G Avenue. The indoor swimming pool cost $10,000 to construct and included 65 individual-sized dressing rooms, a slide, and shallow water for children. Bathing suits cost 25¢ to rent, while gallery admission was free. From 2000 to 2002, the Douglas Area Food Bank rehabilitated the building for its food distribution operation.

The vegetation was lush in the early 1920s when Joe Carlson stood in the patio of Douglas Grammar School. Carlson was the principal of the school; he began serving as superintendent of schools in 1927. Nine years after his retirement in 1948, the school was named after him. It has since been an intermediate school and primary school, and it now contains district offices.

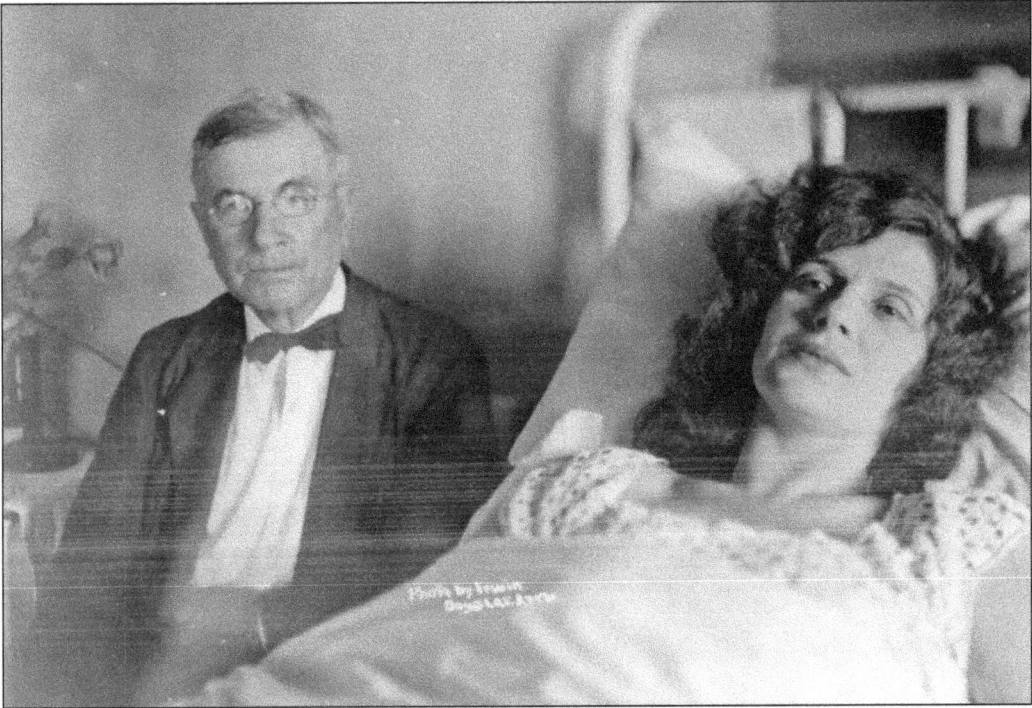

Aimee Semple McPherson was perhaps the most famous American evangelist in 1926, and on May 16 of that year she disappeared. On June 23, she reappeared in Agua Prieta and was whisked away to the Calumet and Arizona Hospital, at 640 Tenth Street, where she was photographed with Douglas mayor A. E. Hinton (above). A media frenzy developed as the evangelist spun a tale of kidnapping and captivity in a Mexican shack. Despite an exhaustive search, the shack was never found, tarnishing McPherson's reputation, but burnishing Douglas's image, as the satirical postcard demonstrates. (Below, author's collection.)

A ceremony on November 7, 1936, marked the opening of the Douglas Underpass, a structure that was the last grade separation on U.S. Highway 80, then one of the principal routes across America. The concrete underpass featured two metal medallions bearing a likeness of Apache leader Cochise. When the underpass was knocked down in 2001 to make way for a modern intersection, the medallions were saved. One is on display at the Douglas Visitors Center and the other on the sign overhang at the intersection entrance.

Two

REVOLUTION!

In the 1800s, Rafael Elías González owned the land where Douglas and Agua Prieta came to be. A great grandson, Plutarco Elías Calles, came to be closely associated with Agua Prieta and the town's prominent role in the Mexican Revolution.

Calles ran an Agua Prieta store before the Mexican Revolution began in November 1910. Until then, no rebellion came close to deposing long-time dictator Porfirio Diaz, but Francisco Madero attempted the impossible.

In April 1911, Madero sympathizers attacked Diaz troops in Agua Prieta. Douglas residents rushed toward the border to watch as the rebels twice defeated federal troops in the first Battle of Agua Prieta. The action helped put Madero in the Mexican president's chair, but he was murdered in 1913, and civil war soon began ravaging Mexico. Regional leaders such as Pancho Villa and Emiliano Zapata battled Constitutionalists led by Venustiano Carranza.

Calles allied with Álvaro Obregón, a fellow Sonoran and constitutionalist general. Calles held Sonora while in central Mexico, and Obregón repeatedly defeated Villa, who retreated to his Chihuahuan stronghold.

Needing to resupply, Villa required control of a town with access to the United States. In October 1915, that town was Agua Prieta. Villa's soldiers marched there and flung themselves against Calles's substantial defenses, which included troops transported on American trains from Juarez–El Paso to Douglas–Agua Prieta.

The second Battle of Agua Prieta lasted two days and, as in 1911, many area residents hurried to the border to watch the fighting. Villa's defeat helped solidify Constitutionalist supremacy, resulting in Carranza becoming president of Mexico.

Villa's anger over American recognition of the Constitutionalists prompted his vengeful raid on Columbus, New Mexico, in 1916. The U.S. response was the Punitive Expedition, in which Douglas soldiers participated.

In 1920, Calles and Obregón supported the Plan de Agua Prieta, a rationale for their revolt against Carranza. Ultimately Obregón assumed the presidency, and Calles followed him. While in power, Calles established the Institutional Revolutionary Party (PRI), which dominated Mexico until 2000. Thus events in Agua Prieta–Douglas affected the course of Mexican history.

Much border-town intrigue occurred during the years leading up to 1910 as rebels sought to end the 26-year reign of dictator Porfirio Diaz. One such rebel in the Douglas–Agua Prieta area was Arturo "Red" Lopez, seen above. On April 13, 1911, he gathered some men, such as those in the photograph below. They commandeered the Nacozari train and used it as a Trojan horse to enter Agua Prieta. The *insurrectos* surprised the Federal garrison that, after a brisk battle, took refuge in Douglas.

Once in control of Agua Prieta, the insurrectos set out guards, including this white-bearded man at right. The Federalists' counterattack occurred on April 15, 1911. By then, the insurrectos were bolstered by American volunteers, such as the men in the photograph below. This combined force successfully repulsed the Federal attack, but the rebels abandoned Agua Prieta a few days later as the Federalists received reinforcements and prepared another assault.

WATCHING THE BATTLE AT AGUA PREITA

Federal Dead

Among those watching the Federal attempt to retake Agua Prieta on April 15, 1911, were these people at 801 Fifth Street (above). There had been so many civilian casualties from stray bullets on April 13 that 1st Cavalry soldiers cleared the area south of Fifth Street—the photograph on the cover is part of this measure. The house in this image was just north of "the dead line." Notice the man standing on the left, viewing the action with a telescope.

During lulls in the 1911 Battle of Agua Prieta, onlookers from Douglas would walk across the borderline to grab souvenirs and gawk at the dead. Douglas physician J. J. P. Armstrong collected 28 different calibers of bullets used by insurrectos during the battle. The men in this photograph are looking at Federal soldiers killed at the bullring, which marked Agua Prieta's eastern edge in 1911.

MOVING FROM AGUA PREITA, MEXICO, INTO THE GOOD OLD U.S.A.

The Mexican Revolution created many refugees, including the men in the photograph above, standing in front the U.S. Customs building in Douglas. In 1912, the increasing violence of the Mexican Revolution forced a large wave of refugees across the border. Among them were Mormon colonists, many of whom settled in Douglas, and whose descendents live in town today. The 1912 exodus did not include Red Lopez. Shortly after the first Battle of Agua Prieta, James Hilburn, a Douglas man who had a cattle ranch south of Agua Prieta, found Lopez's hastily buried body, seen at right.

RED LOPEZ AS FOUND

During the last week of October 1915, the residents of Agua Prieta kept looking east toward Cerro Gallardo, the domed mountain peeking through the power poles in the photograph above. Everyone was watching for the approach of the man in the photograph at left, Pancho Villa. His army, following battlefield defeats by the Constitutionalist faction earlier in 1915, was marching 125 miles from Chihuahua to Agua Prieta to seize what Villa thought was a lightly defended town. He did not know Constitutionalist commander Plutarco Elías Calles had received reinforcements. (Above, courtesy Roy Manley.)

The reinforcements Calles received for his 1915 defense of Agua Prieta against Pancho Villa included artillery pieces, machine guns, and men. The equipment arrived on October 28 and the soldiers on October 30. In the photograph above, Constitutionalist troops march through Agua Prieta, down Fifth Street, and past the Hotel Central, the two-story building to the soldiers' right. The observation tower on the photograph's right side remained intact into the 1940s. Upon their arrival, the soldiers immediately entered defenses such as the breastworks in the photograph below. (Both courtesy Roy Manley.)

33

GALLES ARTILLERY IN ACTION

Villa's attack on Agua Prieta began November 1, 1915, at 1:37 p.m. with an artillery barrage. The Constitutionalists responded with their own guns (above). The same as during the 1911 Battle of Agua Prieta, Douglasites and residents from the surrounding area rushed to the border to watch the action (below). Fewer Americans were killed in 1915 by stray bullets, but there were more injuries. Among the latter were four people named Jones; one of them an army corporal who died of his wound. Camp Douglas was renamed in his honor in 1916. (Above, courtesy Roy Manley.)

WATCHING FIGHT IN AGUA PREITA, FROM DOUGLAS, ARIZ.
(DOUBLEDAY)

These Agua Prieta youngsters are pointing out some of the damage caused by Villista (Pancho Villa supporters) artillery shells fired during the 1915 Battle of Agua Prieta. Much of the cannonade was aimed into the central portion of town where Calles had his quarters and office. Villa's main attempt to capture Agua Prieta took place after dark on November 1, with sporadic attacks throughout November 2. The Villistas initially attacked from the east and gradually swung around the southern rim of Agua Prieta. The final attempt to enter Agua Prieta came from the west, but the Constitutionalist defenders in trenches and behind barbed wire proved resilient.

The photograph above was taken at Naco, Sonora, but is included here because it provides evidence that the town west of Agua Prieta is where Calles learned the value of World War I–style defensive tactics. Trenches and barbed wire were crucial in Naco's defense as well as in Agua Prieta. The futility of the Villista effort in Agua Prieta is best illustrated below by the line of dead horses strewn in front of barbed-wire entanglements that were in clear view of the Copper Queen and Calumet and Arizona smelters. Villa's defeat at Agua Prieta reduced him from a national power back to just a regional leader. (Both courtesy Roy Manley.)

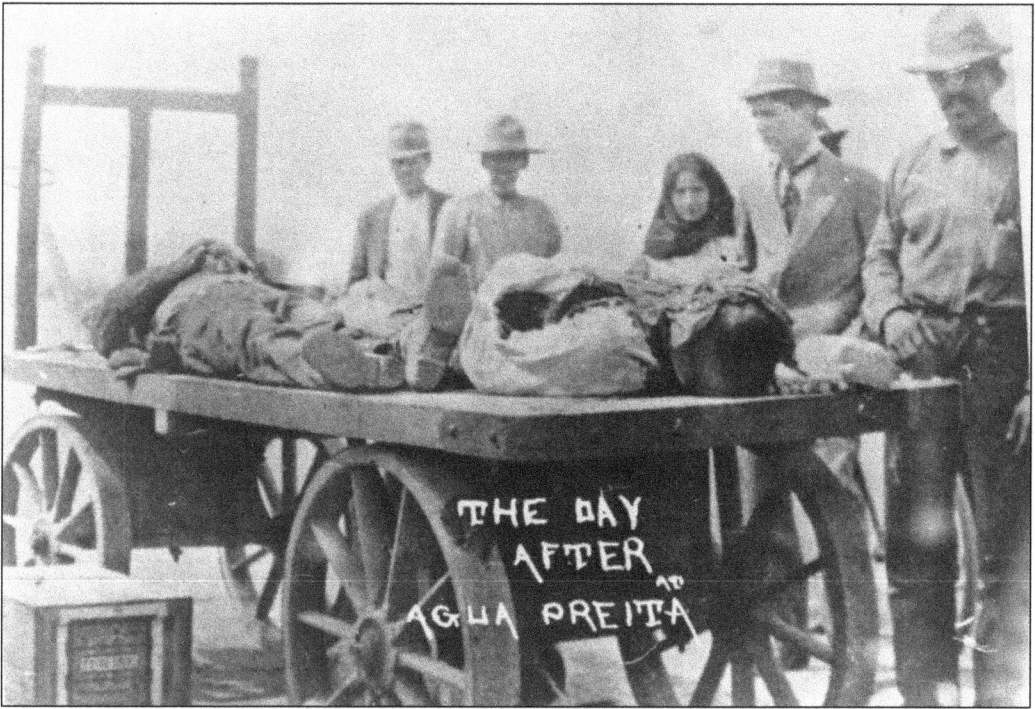

There were more casualties among Mexican troops, especially Villistas, during the 1915 Battle of Agua Prieta than in the 1911 battle. There were so many dead in 1915 that, unless bodies were claimed, they were heaped into piles and burned before the cremains were buried in mass graves.

Whether a Mexican soldier or an American soldier in 1916, the routine for the enlisted man was much the same—hurry up and wait. (Below, courtesy Roy Manley.)

Alice Gatliff was an American businesswoman who lived in Agua Prieta. The photograph on the right was taken about the time of the 1915 Battle of Agua Prieta. She is holding a baby burro. The photograph below shows her standing in front of her Agua Prieta compound, on the northeast corner of Second Street and Fifth Avenue. It housed her saloon, restaurant, curio store, and lodging rooms. One of her pastimes was photography, and the images on the next page are almost certainly her work.

This photograph shows Plutarco Elías Calles (in white shirt), the commander at Agua Prieta in 1915. To the left is Max Joffre, a Chilean military advisor (holding hat). The man wearing glasses is Calles's aide-de-camp, Joaquín Amaro. The other two men are unidentified. (Courtesy Roy Manley.)

In this photograph taken April 23, 1920, Gen. Plutarco Elías Calles (left) is reading the Plan de Agua Prieta, a rationale for armed revolt against Mexican president Venustiano Carranza. Calles and his listeners signed the plan on the table under Calles's elbow, which was in Alice Gatliff's Curio Café. The revolt ended with Álvaro Obregón in the president's chair, followed by Calles. During his time as Mexico's leader, Calles founded the Partido Revolucionario Institucional (Institutional Revolutionary Party), the political party that produced every Mexican president until 2000. (Courtesy Armando Elías.)

Three

MILITARY

Douglas was the site of two major U.S. Army installations. The first took shape during autumn of 1910 when fears that the Mexican Revolution would spill into the United States brought about demands for army protection.

This took the form of a cavalry detachment. The soldiers camped inside Sportsmen's Park and guarded the border during the first Battle of Agua Prieta.

That action plus civilian casualties meant more soldiers came to Douglas. Eventually a camp sprawled from Sixth to Fifteenth Streets and from Florida Avenue onto land now occupied by Douglas Municipal Airport. Other facilities included a firing range, where the current rifle range is now, and an outpost at John Slaughter's ranch, 15 miles east of town. Units regularly tramped there as a field exercise.

On November 2, 1915, during the second Battle of Agua Prieta, a stray bullet wounded Cpl. Harry J. Jones, and he died the next day. A request to name the camp after Jones became official February 18, 1916.

The next month, as part of the U.S. response to Villa's Columbus raid, the 6th Field Artillery left Camp Jones as part of the Punitive Expedition. The Columbus raid also caused activation of National Guard companies. During the summer of 1916, Douglas hosted several units.

After the United States entered World War I, Camp Jones became a brigade headquarters. This meant over 5,000 soldiers lived there and trained for overseas duty.

Camp Jones held an army border patrol district headquarters beginning in 1920, and it was not closed until 1932. Little remains of Camp Jones today but photographs.

During the first six months of 1942, Douglas Army Air Field was rapidly built 10 miles north of Douglas. The base was a twin-engine flight school for officers assigned to bombers during World War II. Thousands trained in Douglas before going overseas.

After World War II, the army airfield became Bisbee-Douglas Airport, where hangars held a variety of postwar businesses. The airport was on the American Airlines schedule into the early 1960s.

CAMP OF U.S. CAV. DOUGLAS, ARIZ.

DOUBLEDAY - HEUTHER

During autumn of 1910, a detachment of about 100 First Cavalry soldiers rode into Douglas to protect the town from any incursions of Mexican Revolution activity. Initially the solders camped inside Sportsmen Park; that is the outfield fence behind the tents in the photograph above. As the Mexican Revolution grew, so did Camp Douglas. Rows of its tents stretch to the horizon in the photograph below, taken about 1915.

Chow call in Camp Douglas was at 7:00 a.m., noon, and 5:00 p.m. The men in the photograph above must be lining up for lunch. A distinctive smell at Camp Douglas emanated from the dozens of bubbling troop kitchen incinerators, seen below. (Courtesy Douglas Historical Society.)

Weather extremes were part of life at Camp Douglas. In the photograph above, infantry soldiers led by mounted officers are on the go in summer heat. A common field exercise was marching to Slaughter's ranch, east of Douglas, for a several weeks' stay. Between January 19 and 21, 1916, a foot of snow fell on Douglas and its army camp, pictured below. Roofs of several Douglas buildings collapsed under the weight of accumulated snow. (Above, courtesy Roy Manley.)

Soldiers stationed at Douglas often "showed the flag" by participating in parades. In the photograph above, an infantry unit marches past Phelps Dodge Mercantile while sharing G Avenue with a streetcar. In the photograph below, Batteries B and C of the Sixth Field Artillery march in a Liberty Bond parade on G Avenue. The two batteries participated in the Punitive Expedition into Mexico, and Battery C fired the first American round in France on October 20, 1917. (Above, courtesy Roy Manley.)

During a World War I–era expansion, many tents at Camp Jones were taken down, as in this photograph, and replaced by single-story, wooden barracks. The buildings in the photograph on the bottom of page 43 are an example of this type of cantonment. (Courtesy Douglas Historical Society.)

On January 31, 1920, Gen. John "Black Jack" Pershing visited Douglas and Camp Jones. The general spoke to former servicemen inside the Elks Club, at 650 Tenth Street, before going onto the building's balcony and addressing the public. The crowd was a large one, as this photograph shows. Perhaps Pershing's influence helped Camp Jones remain open through the 1920s, but when the Great Depression set in during the early 1930s, Camp Jones closed permanently. Many of its houses and other buildings were moved. For instance, the building today at 1527 F Avenue used to be the Camp Jones chapel. (Courtesy Douglas Historical Society.)

During the first six months of 1942, Douglas Army Air Field took shape 10 miles north of town. Notice the airplanes lined up on the apron in this aerial photograph taken in 1943. Facilities included a theater, post office, and hospital in addition to quarters, service clubs, and a gymnasium.

This group of aviation cadets at Douglas Army Air Field was from Great Britain. In addition to thousands of American aviators, pilots from Nationalist China also trained at the field. Late in World War II, when fighter pilots were no longer in high demand, some men retrained as bomber pilots at Douglas, including a few of the famed Tuskegee Airmen. (Courtesy Douglas Historical Society.)

Many cadets at Douglas Army Air Field learned how to fly twin-engine planes in this type of aircraft. To civilians, it was a Beechcraft B-18; to those in the military, it was an AT-11. This particular plane has a turret on top for gunnery training and a clear nose for bombardier training.

In 1943, the 953rd Engineers Topographic Company cleared brush and set up their tents east of Florida Avenue between Eleventh and Twelfth Streets. The engineers' duty involved aerial-map analysis, and they arranged to have their camp photographed.

Four

AVIATION

A history of Douglas aviation includes this list of firsts:

first heavier-than-air craft in Arizona, a glider pulled aloft in early 1908
first powered plane designed and built in Arizona (the glider motorized), 1910
first international military flight (from Douglas into revolutionary Mexico), 1913
first regular military aircraft to land in Arizona, 1916
first aerial border patrol station, 1920
first National Aeronautics Association chapter in Arizona, 1927

Members of that chapter brought about construction of Douglas Municipal Airport in 1928. It has its own list of firsts:

first international airport in the Americas, 1929
first lighted airport in southwest (before Los Angeles and El Paso), 1932
first use of federal funds to build Arizona airport facilities (a hangar), 1930
on one of the first regularly scheduled passenger service routes, 1929
a stop on the first National Women's Air (Powder Puff) Derby, 1929
on the first regularly scheduled federal airmail service route, 1930

After World War II, Douglas Army Air Field became Bisbee-Douglas Airport, which hosted various businesses, including the Trojan airplane factory. The sturdy, two-seater airplanes were constructed in Douglas during 1949–1950.

Today a Trojan airplane resides in a small museum built by Richard Westbrook, a Douglas native, after his retirement as a NASA engineer. The museum, at Douglas Municipal Airport, is open to the public.

A third Douglas-area airfield is on the Cochise College campus. The college's highly regarded pilot, avionic, and mechanic programs were established in the 1960s.

On February 26, 1910, Charles K. Hamilton took off in his Curtiss biplane from Sportsmens Park. It was the third air show ever held in Arizona, and it attracted thousands of people, including 750 from Bisbee. They had taken advantage of a special offer in the Bisbee Miner—round-trip train fare to Douglas, admission to the show, and a month's subscription to the newspaper—all for $2. The ballpark fence and Saddlegap Mountain are in the background. (Courtesy Douglas Historical Society.)

Glendale, California–based Pickwick Airlines existed only from 1928 until 1930, but Douglas was on its schedule. This plane and its gasoline truck are at the brand-new Douglas Municipal Airport in this photograph. Standard Airlines, another pioneer aviation company, began sending its 14-passenger, trimotor Fokker planes to Douglas in 1929. (Courtesy Douglas Historical Society.)

The first regularly scheduled coast-to-coast airmail service in the United States began on October 15, 1930. Three planes took off carrying sacks of mail; two of them stopped in Douglas. Posing in this photograph are, from left to right, William Jackson, assistant Douglas postmaster; Edward Huxtable, Douglas postmaster; John Crowell, Bank of Douglas manager; Frank Hitchcock, former U.S. postmaster general; Guy Crouch, Owl Drug Store owner; Earle Ovington, pilot; Nicolas Arvela, Agua Prieta postmaster; and Blanche Shotwell, Douglas Post Office employee.

In the years immediately following World War II, local authorities took over Douglas Army Air Field, renaming it Bisbee-Douglas Airport. In 1948, American Airlines began regular flights to the airport. At the ribbon-cutting ceremony for the first flight are, from left to right, Everett J. Jones, Douglas mayor; A. B. Bone, American Airlines vice president; and Glendora Otis, an American Airlines stewardess who grew up in Douglas. Her father, Charles Otis, managed the JCPenney store and was president of the chamber of commerce. American Airlines included Bisbee-Douglas on its schedule into the early 1960s.

Early in 1949, Harold E. Emigh (pronounced "Amy") moved his Trojan Airplane factory from California to Douglas. Most of the two-seat, all-metal craft, which were noteworthy because of Emigh's simple, study design, emerged from this assembly line in a Bisbee-Douglas Airport hangar. The airplanes' price range was from $2,695 to $3,295.

During October 1949, the well-known aviator Mardo Crane flew the *City of Douglas* Trojan airplane from Arizona to Chicago on a publicity tour. Former mayor Everett J. Jones saw her off. Despite Crane's effort, a severely depressed market for private aircraft shut down the factory in 1950. Only 59 Trojans were built and only 17 exist today. One is at Douglas Municipal Airport in a small museum that is open to the public.

Five

TRANSPORTATION AND TOURISM

Life in Douglas depended upon its railroads. Copper concentrate from Bisbee and Nacozari rolled into town, along with New Mexico coal and coke to fuel smelter furnaces. Copper anodes left, as did cars filled with cattle from ranches on both sides of the international border.

Some days, six to eight trains flowed in and out of Douglas, which was an El Paso and Southwestern Railroad section headquarters. The railroad's roundhouse, shops, warehouses, and passenger depot dominated Douglas's west side.

In 1903, a streetcar system began taking workers to the smelters. Trolleys traveled the length of Tenth Street, Fourth and Sixteenth Streets, A and G Avenues, and through the Fairview addition past Pirtleville.

Streetcar operations ceased in 1920. One factor was the automobile. As early as 1913, Douglas called itself "Auto Town of the Southwest" and claimed over 200 automobiles. Street paving started in 1917.

In 1920, the road between Bisbee and Douglas became the first hard-surfaced highway in Arizona. That year, Cochise County had the second-largest number of cars in Arizona with over 3,500.

The Bisbee-Douglas Road became part of the Bankhead Highway, one of the first transcontinental thoroughfares. Its route between Washington, D.C., and San Diego made the Bankhead Highway popular with tourists. Businessmen promoted Douglas as a tourist destination, capitalizing on closeness to Mexico, where liquor still flowed during Prohibition.

The Gadsden Hotel, built in 1907 as Douglas's showpiece, benefitted from this, especially after it was rebuilt following a 1928 fire. The hotel's competition was tourist camps.

The first such in the country was Askins Cottage Camp, established in the 700 block of Seventeenth Street before 1924. Several similar camps followed and flourished until the 1950s when the interstate highway moved to Willcox.

Dominance of automotive traffic affected railroads too. Ridership declined so much that Southern Pacific halted passenger trains to Douglas in 1961. With cessation of Bisbee copper mining in 1978, there was little need for the railroad to Douglas. Tracks between Douglas and Paul Spur were removed in the 1990s.

Three different types of transportation appear in this c. 1920 photograph showing the intersection of G Avenue and Tenth Street. The end of a streetcar can be seen on Tenth Street between the Bank of Douglas and the Douglas Drug Store, which was then two stories tall. A horse-drawn wagon passes by a race car (notice the number painted on the hood) parked in front of the Bellevue Hotel, at 1013 G Avenue. Notice also the soldiers lounging at the Arcade Pool Hall under the hotel. Parked passenger cars line both sides of G Avenue. (Courtesy Roy Manley.)

The fascination of many Douglas residents with the automobile resulted in the town being part of numerous races. Some events were cross-country; others took place on Douglas's racetrack. This stripped-down race car parked, with an unknown driver and passenger, is in front of the Cochise Overland Company office, at 936–940 F Avenue, at an unknown date. The building later became the Coca-Cola bottling plant. (Courtesy Roy Manley.)

In the 1920s and 1930s, the Douglas automotive racetrack was west of the YMCA building, which can be seen on the end of the racetrack that is partially cut off in this aerial photograph. To the right of the YMCA building, down Railroad Avenue, is a long, rectangular, dark-roofed building. This was the Southern Pacific Railroad freight warehouse. West of the warehouse are several buildings. The largest, a rectangular structure with a light-colored roof, is the Sonora Mercantile building. Run by the Haymore family, it housed the Haymore Feed Store during the 1970s and 1980s. The dark building between the Haymore building and the freight warehouse was the Copper City Brewing/People's Ice plant (page 14). The white buildings south of the Haymore building were where the Arizona Gypsum Plaster Company manufactured Litholite hard-wall plaster and pure-gypsum hollow blocks, which the company sold into the 1940s.

As a section headquarters for the El Paso and Southwestern Railroad, and as a division point for other railroads, Douglas naturally became the site of locomotive and car servicing facilities. A 15-stall roundhouse was built west of Railroad Avenue between Thirteenth and Fourteenth

Physical labor was part of the job description for many railroad workers, including these men moving car wheels. In the panoramic photograph at the top of the page, notice the stick protruding from the right side of the turntable. The men clustered at the table used the stick and another inserted in the other end of the table to rotate it before the tender on the left moved cars onto the proper tracks. (Courtesy Douglas Historical Society.)

Streets. Grouped nearby were a turntable, section house, machine shop, master mechanic's office, sand house, coal bunkers, and cinder pits. Roundhouse work stopped in 1963. (Courtesy Roy Manley.)

The Douglas passenger depot is a Beaux Arts–style building with a central rotunda and porticos on its east and west sides. Erected in 1913, the building greeted thousands of passengers, especially during World War II when troop trains passed through Douglas. John Salem created the unique sign, which went into storage about the time passenger service ceased in 1961. In 1993, the sign returned to its former location when the depot was rehabilitated into the Douglas Police Station, earning the Governor's Award for Historic Preservation.

Although the date of its founding is not known exactly, Askins Cottage Camp, in the 700 block of Seventeenth Street, is considered the country's first tourist court (motel). Consisting of one-room cabins connected by carports with a community wash house and kitchen, the Askins camp (above) and others, such as the Rest-A-Bit Tourist Lodge, at 502 Sixteenth Street, attracted tourists motoring over America's rapidly improving roadways in the 1920s. The Bisbee-Douglas Road led the way when it was dedicated in 1920 as the first hard-surfaced highway in the state. (Above, courtesy Douglas Historical Society; below, Roy Manley.)

Hailed as the finest hostelry between El Paso and Los Angeles, the Gadsden Hotel opened in 1907. By 1928, however, the four-story building needed renovation, which its new owners, Franklin and Mary Mackey, started. On February 8, at 5:12 a.m., a milkman spotted smoke. Water was pouring on the building less than four minutes later, but the blaze grew quickly, and firefighters concentrated on keeping the fire from spreading to the adjacent Phelps Dodge Mercantile (above). No one was injured, but losses totaled almost $275,000, and the Gadsden was a ruin (below).

The Gadsden Hotel's main entrance faced Eleventh Street in the 1920s. A light-colored portico marked the G Avenue entrance. In the lobby's center was a bronze created by famous French artist Isidore Bonheur. The sculpture portrayed a steeplechase on Paris's Longchamp course and was the property of James S. Douglas, who developed an appreciation of French art while working there for the Red Cross during World War I. The statue was the first object removed during the 1928 fire and the first returned in 1929.

The Mackeys rebuilt the Gadsden with two major changes. They added a fifth floor and rotated the building so its main entrance faced G Avenue instead of Eleventh Street, as seen above in the 1960s. The photograph below features the main staircase with a custom oil painting and art glass adorning the east mezzanine wall. The Gadsden has long been "the living room of Douglas," says Robin Brekhus, whose family currently owns the hotel. (Both courtesy Holly Berryhill.)

The Gadsden bar became famous for its wall decorations—brands of Cochise County ranches as well as some nationally known spreads. The Gadsden bar and the B&P Palace, across G Avenue, were the sites of many a handshake cattle purchase or other business deal. (Courtesy Holly Berryhill.)

While rebuilding the Gadsden, Franklin Mackey decided to add a storage and service garage at 427 Eleventh Street, west of his hotel. The storage option was especially popular during Prohibition when hotel guests went to Agua Prieta, where liquor and gambling were readily available. A red, white, and blue map showing the entire length of U.S. Highway 80, painted on the wall facing the gasoline pumps, was the garage's trademark. George and Fred Fleetham acquired the garage in 1943 and kept it open 24 hours a day, seven days a week, until 1975. After the Fleethams sold the building, it was torn down to enlarge a parking lot.

Six

SMELTERS

Calumet and Arizona, a Michigan company, and Copper Queen Mining, a Phelps Dodge and Company subsidiary, both built smelters in Douglas. Copper Queen executives decided where the town would be, but the C&A got its smelter running first, on November 15, 1902.

The Copper Queen smelter became operational during March 1903 and then expanded rapidly. In 1908, it produced 40,000 tons per month, making it the world's second-largest smelter.

Ore mined in Bisbee and Nacozari was concentrated there. In Douglas, the smelting process began with roasters and reverbatory furnaces, followed by convertors. In those devices, air blew through the molten mass to refine it, which was then poured into moulds. After cooling, those anodes were shipped to a refinery.

One important addition to the smelting process was lime, supplied by Alfred Paul from his quarry 10 miles west of Douglas. The community of Paul Spur grew up near the crushers and kiln.

World War I created an unprecedented demand for copper. Both smelters were ready, having installed new equipment during 1912–1913. The Copper Queen produced almost 21 million pounds of copper in January 1918 alone.

Smelting this much copper required a large workforce. About 1,600 people worked at the CQ, and 700 worked at the C&A. Combined with 600 railroad workers, Douglas's civilian population rose to 18,000 in 1917.

An economic recession followed World War I, temporarily closing both smelters. But conditions soon improved enough that in 1927, Phelps Dodge built a small smelter for custom work.

Douglas's third smelter was dedicated on August 18, 1927, but its operating life was short. The Great Depression closed all three smelters; only one reopened.

On September 21, 1931, the Calumet and Arizona merged into Phelps Dodge. The C&A smelter became the Douglas Reduction Works. Eventually the Copper Queen smelters were razed and forgotten.

Douglas Reduction Works kept running after Nacozari all but shut down in 1949, and after Bisbee's mines closed from 1976 to 1978. The smelter cast its last anodes in 1987.

Dismantling began in 1989 and the smokestacks, which marked the Douglas skyline for 85 years, came down in 1991.

Underground mines in Nacozari and Bisbee supplied the material sent to Douglas for smelting until 1951 when work began on the Lavender Pit, which has only five benches in this photograph. Bisbee is visible in the back mountains, and Lowell is the suburb in the foreground. Following extraction, ore from the pit, containing as little as one percent copper or less, went through a series of crushing devices that ground it into powder. In concentrator (large building on right) flotation cells, the powder, water, pine oil, and other materials were gently agitated. The resulting concentrate, around 28 percent copper, was loaded into railroad cars that traveled to Douglas daily. (Author's collection.)

Paul Lime Company, begun by Alfred Paul in 1902, provided lime needed by the Copper Queen and Calumet and Arizona Mining Companies in their Bisbee and Douglas operations. The Paul Lime plant included a quarry, crushers, and kiln, which heated the limestone, thus turning it into lime. This photograph shows the horizontal kiln in which heated limestone slowly rotates. Paul family members sold the plant in 1971, and it remains in operation today under management of an international corporation.

At the Copper Queen smelter, railroad cars dumped concentrate into bedding troughs. These were east of the smelter in the light-colored area of this aerial photograph. Douglas is in the upper right corner of the photograph. The smallest smoke stack (center) serviced the powerhouse, the light-colored building to the right of the small stack. After this smelter closed about 1936, the powerhouse became a warehouse, and today it is the most visible remnant of the Copper Queen smelter.

Assayers, such as the man in this photograph, analyzed samples taken from the bedding area to calculate ore percentage and the amount of silica and lime, which were mixed into the concentrate in order to produce the most purely refined copper possible. (Courtesy Douglas Historical Society.)

For the first 30 or so years of production, Bisbee had largely oxide-type ores, but around 1910 miners began encountering sulfide ore. This ore required an extra processing step, roasting, to drive off the sulfur. In 1912, the Calumet and Arizona began construction of roasters on the eastern portion of its Douglas smelter. Workers completed all foundation work by hand, as this photograph attests.

Roasted concentrate, or calcine, next entered a reverbatory furnace. This is the interior of a reverbatory shortly after construction was completed. Within its confines, 2,500-degree Fahrenheit heat initiated chemical reactions within the concentrate. This produced a matte of about 60 percent copper and a waste product known as slag. The slag floated on top of the lava-like matte in the furnace and was skimmed off and poured into slag pots for disposal. (Author's collection.)

Slag pots, filled with molten waste material, were dumped in an ever-widening arc around the smelter. The orange cascades of slag hardened in a black mass that is one of the most inert materials known to mankind. Crushed slag stabilized railroad track beds, was purchased to fill private driveways, and mixed with asphalt to pave highways. In this photograph, probably taken about 1910, the slag-train locomotive is steam powered. In later years, the train was electrically powered.

The photograph above provides an exterior view of the Copper Queen's convertor building, where the next step in the smelting process took place. The pipes arcing into the convertor roof were a distinctive feature of this smelter for its whole life and of the Calumet and Arizona smelter for many years. Inside the convertor building (apparently undergoing construction in the photograph below), the pipes attached to each convertor furnace and blew in air at low pressure. The combination of high temperature and steady air draft is called a reducing atmosphere, and it produced blister copper—around 98 percent pure—and a slag.

Following the 1931 merger of Phelps Dodge and the Calumet and Arizona, the latter's smelter became the Douglas Reduction Works, and the Copper Queen smelter closed. There were operational changes too. Blister copper was poured into ladles (above), as was slag, by means of an overhead crane running the length of the convertor aisle. The convertor slag went into pots (below) to be recycled into the reverbatory furnaces.

In an anode furnace, high-pressure air is shot through the blister copper, removing most of the remaining impurities. By the time the copper is poured out of the furnace into moulds, it is 99.4 percent pure (above). Sixteen moulds rim a large casting wheel. Each mould produces an anode, which, after cooling slightly, is pulled out of the wheel with the large tongs hanging from a chain, which the operator is holding (below).

Following removal from the wheel, anodes are dunked in water to cool them rapidly (above). Then they are stacked in long rows (below) to await shipment to the Phelps Dodge refinery in El Paso, Texas. Each anode weighs approximately 750 pounds and has "ears" for ease of handling with a forklift. In the refinery, the anodes are suspended from their ears in fluid-filled tanks and electrically charged to produce cathodes of 99.99 percent pure copper that are then manufactured into electrical wire and other useful objects.

About half the heat emanating from the Douglas Reduction Works reverbatory furnaces was captured by a smokestack flue and routed to steam-generating boilers. The steam went to electrical generators. Two such generators are on the right side of this c. 1940 photograph. Behind the generators is a flywheel whose spinning produced enough current so that if a power failure occurred, two things could happen: the mass in the convertors could be turned out so as not to solidify inside, and secondly, the convertor crane could run to the end of the aisle so the operator could get out. On the left side of the photograph are three blowers, which sent air to the convertors. Behind them is an air compressor for pneumatic tools.

In the 1920s, water not used up in the steam-powered electrical generators at the Calumet and Arizona smelter went into a cooling pond. Smelter superintendent Harry Clark allowed the public to use the pond, which was a popular swimming pool despite its lukewarm water.

One part of the Douglas Reduction Works was this sponge iron plant. As its name implies, sponge iron has a porous structure, which made it an ideal component of a process called cementation. Nacozari's underground mines stopped producing rock ore in 1949, but they kept producing copper via cementation. In this process, mine water laden with copper in solution is gathered and brought into contact with specially prepared sponge iron, resulting in copper leachate. In this way, Nacozari produced copper for 15 years after traditional mining ceased. (Author's collection.)

In the late 1960s and 1970s, increasing environmental awareness brought about increasing pressure on Douglas Reduction Works to reduce pollution. Two Phelps Dodge efforts to do so are shown here. Hoods were placed over convertors (left) to catch escaping gases, and electrostatic precipitators (below) were installed to capture particulate matter that otherwise would go up the stack. (Both author's collection.)

Under a half moon, the Douglas Reduction Works glows with its own light. Most of the people who lived in Douglas when this smelter was operational recognized the smoke coming out of the stacks and the slag pouring down the dump (bright flare on the left) represented the town's lifeblood. (Courtesy Douglas Historical Society.)

Dr. James Douglas (above left) tried several professions before inventing the first electrolytic method of refining copper. This plus a keen mind kept him in demand as a consultant, and in this capacity he recommended Phelps Dodge and Company purchase copper mines in the Southwest and Mexico. Both of Dr. Douglas's sons followed him into prominent positions with Phelps Dodge. James S. Douglas (upper right) became superintendent of the company's Nacozari operation and then president of United Verde Company in Jerome, Arizona. James's son Lewis Douglas (left) was Arizona's Congressman between 1926 and 1932, Franklin Roosevelt's first budget director, and an ambassador to England. Dr. Douglas's other son, Walter (not shown), was a vice president, general manager, and director with Phelps Dodge. (All author's collection.)

In 1910, Stuart French (above right) succeeded Walter Douglas as general manager of the Copper Queen Company, overseeing Bisbee mines and Douglas smelter. During 26 years with Phelps Dodge, P. G. Beckett (above left) was western operations general manager and a company vice president. Harry A. Clark (right) was superintendent of the Calumet and Arizona smelter, and he remained in that position after the C&A merged with Phelps Dodge in 1931. All three began their professional careers in other fields or with other copper companies before finding a niche within Phelps Dodge. The company gained renown for its managers' consistent professionalism and altruistic attitude. For example, French was a regional Boy Scout director, while his wife, Nellie, was the first resident teacher of the Bahá'í Faith in Arizona. (All author's collection.)

In 1927, Phelps Dodge constructed a small smelter between its plant and the Calumet and Arizona works. Before the custom smelter became operational on August 19, a dinner was held inside the smokestack for the men who designed the smelter and oversaw its construction. The author's grandfather John H. Davis Sr. is the second man from the entryway on the outside of the circle. This smelter operated only five years before the Great Depression closed it. (Author's collection.)

The Douglas Reduction Works was the subject of this photograph taken in the late 1950s. It can be dated to that time because the stack of the 1927 smelter still stands on the far right. "Powder men" from the Bisbee mine came to Douglas, set charges around the base of the stack, and imploded it about 1958. (Courtesy Holly Berryhill.)

The steps described in the preceding pages in which copper was produced in a reducing atmosphere—ore crushing, floating, roasting, smelting, and refining—became obsolete in the 1960s. A Finnish firm, Outokumpu Oy, invented a flash smelting process, which had fewer steps and created less pollution than the traditional smelting process. In 1976, Phelps Dodge used Outokumpu equipment to build the Hidalgo smelter in southwestern New Mexico. Phelps Dodge also built the town of Playas (not visible) for employees and their families. These families never saw smelter smoke since Hidalgo captured 95 percent of its sulfur and particulate emissions. (Author's collection.)

Seven

AGRICULTURE

Douglas has long been a focal point for area ranchers and farmers. One reason was early Douglasites and army camp soldiers provided a ready market for agriculturalists.

Farmers sold hay consumed by cavalry horses, as well as vegetables and dairy products consumed by soldiers. Ranchers sold meat to the army.

A few ranchers also sold their beef in Douglas stores, which they owned. One rancher who had this arrangement was John Slaughter, former Cochise County sheriff, whose ranch was 15 miles east of town and whose store was at 525 Tenth Street.

Another reason Douglas became an agricultural center was the railroad, which made shipping easy. The railroad meant that the only Wild West–style cattle drives went to Douglas.

Wild West–style rustling, however, was a problem and cattlemen demanded assistance. They got it in the form of the Arizona Rangers, who headquartered in Douglas between 1903 and 1909.

Cattle owners also formed associations to advance their business. One such group, begun in 1939, was the Cowbelles. Composed of ranchers' wives who initially met to socialize, the Cowbelles grew steadily and is now a national organization deeply involved in beef industry promotion.

Area farmers first depended solely upon rainfall. Around 1910, some began irrigating from wells. Sorghum then, as now, was a popular crop.

After World War II, many farmers from Texas and the Midwest moved to Cochise County. Lettuce gained favor as did chile peppers. Several local facilities sprang up to process chiles.

Although a marginal crop because of the climate, numerous Cochise County farmers received federal subsidies by planting cotton. Recently many switched to specialty crops.

Most area farmers remaining in place following the 1980s farm crisis tended to be those who had been in the business for generations. The same holds true for ranchers; some of whom are now in their sixth generation in Cochise County.

For these families, the Cochise County Fair, with grounds just north of Douglas, is a highlight of the year. Begun in 1921, the fair continues to showcase field crops, livestock, and 4-H and FFA competitors—a reflection of Douglas's farm/ranch heritage.

Among those providing food to early-day Douglasites was Lizzie Leake, seen here in her vegetable patch. Lizzie and her family walked from Fort Stockton, Texas, to Douglas in 1902 and homesteaded on the northern end of King's Highway. Lizzie peddled eggs and chickens in Douglas for 30 years. In 1962, she was honored as the only person in Arizona still living on her original homestead.

Raising poultry was a popular option for many homesteaders and farmers in the Sulphur Springs Valley around Douglas. It was so popular that from January 15 to 17, 1925, the Cochise County Poultry Association held a show for birds judged according to the *American Standard of Perfection*, and for utility birds. Entry fees ranged from 50¢ to $2, and numerous local merchants donated cash or merchandise as prizes.

Cotton was first grown in the Sulphur Springs Valley in 1920, but it did not become a major crop until after World War II (above). In the late 1940s, chile peppers also gained popularity as a crop, perhaps because they were advertised in unique fashion by Mary McDonald (right). The daughter of Kelis McDonald, Mary wore a two-piece swimsuit covered with dried chile peppers for this 1948 promotional photograph.

The water to raise cotton and chiles in Cochise County came from wells that tapped into the groundwater. A few wells, such as the one at left on John Slaughter's ranch, needed little encouragement to become artesian. Slaughter's ranch originally was a Spanish land grant that he acquired in the 1880s. Family members managed the ranch while Slaughter served as sheriff of Cochise County during from 1886 to 1890. Then he retired to his ranch and turned it into a showplace, which always welcomed friends, guests, and family, including Slaughter's grandchildren, who he holds in the photograph below.

Slaughter was called "Texas John" for his origins in the Louisiana-Texas borderlands and his style of raising cattle in Arizona. The so-called Texas system put cattle in large pastures where they cared for themselves year-round. Upon reaching grass-fed maturity, the horned cattle went to market at four years of age. Cowboys used lassos to manage cattle, as seen in these two photographs taken on Slaughter's ranch.

In the 1900s, new cattle-handling methods, such as the chute in the photograph above, took hold on Slaughter's ranch. But the old system of cowboys taking orders from a foreman who got instructions from the ranch owner remained in place. In the photograph below, the owner is Slaughter (left) with his poker-playing friends Hugh Conlon (center), a former Cochise County sheriff, and B. A. Packard, who ranched in Cochise County with Slaughter since the 1880s.

The railroad serving Douglas allowed area ranchers to ship cattle to distant markets without long cattle drives. This eliminated scenes such as the photograph above of a chuck wagon meal. The railroad created scenes such as the one below of the holding pens on the western edge of Douglas that were south of U.S. Highway 80. Notice the cattle are all Herefords—not longhorns—a change promoted by B. A. Packard, who was famous for his purebred stock.

Carton of Flies

Screwworms were blight for area cattlemen until the 1960s. Screwworms are the larvae of a fly that lays its eggs in wounds, unhealed belly buttons, or other skin breaks of any living creature. The larvae eat the flesh of the living creature, maiming or killing it before they turn into pupae. Scientists discovered irradiating male screwworm flies rendered them sterile, thus eventually eliminating the pest. Sterile flies, bred in U.S. Department of Agriculture facilities, were packed in cardboard boxes (above) and dispersed from planes (below). One such facility was at Bisbee-Douglas Airport during the 1960s and 1970s. The program moved south into Mexico in the early 1980s, and screwworms are no longer found in the United States, Mexico, or most Central American countries.

On October 17, 1939, sixteen wives of Douglas-area cattlemen and cattle buyers formed a social club they called the Cowbelles. In order to promote "friendly and social relations between cattle people and to cooperate for the best interests of our industry, our community and our country," the Cowbelles participated in events such as this 1957 rodeo parade, passing in front of the Kazal Brothers Grocery at 560 Tenth Street. Today Cowbelles is a national organization promoting independent cattlemen, their lifestyle, and the beef industry. (Courtesy Douglas Cowbelles.)

The Krentz family, which established a ranch in the San Bernardino Valley east of Douglas in 1907, is an example of the deep roots of many area ranch families today. Several generations of young Krentzes participated in 4-H and Future Farmers of America activities, including Phil Krentz showing his steer in this c. 1960 photograph at the Cochise County Fair. Phil's niece Kyle is a fifth-generation Cowbelle, and Kyle's mother, Susan, was a state president of Cowbelles. (Courtesy Krentz family.)

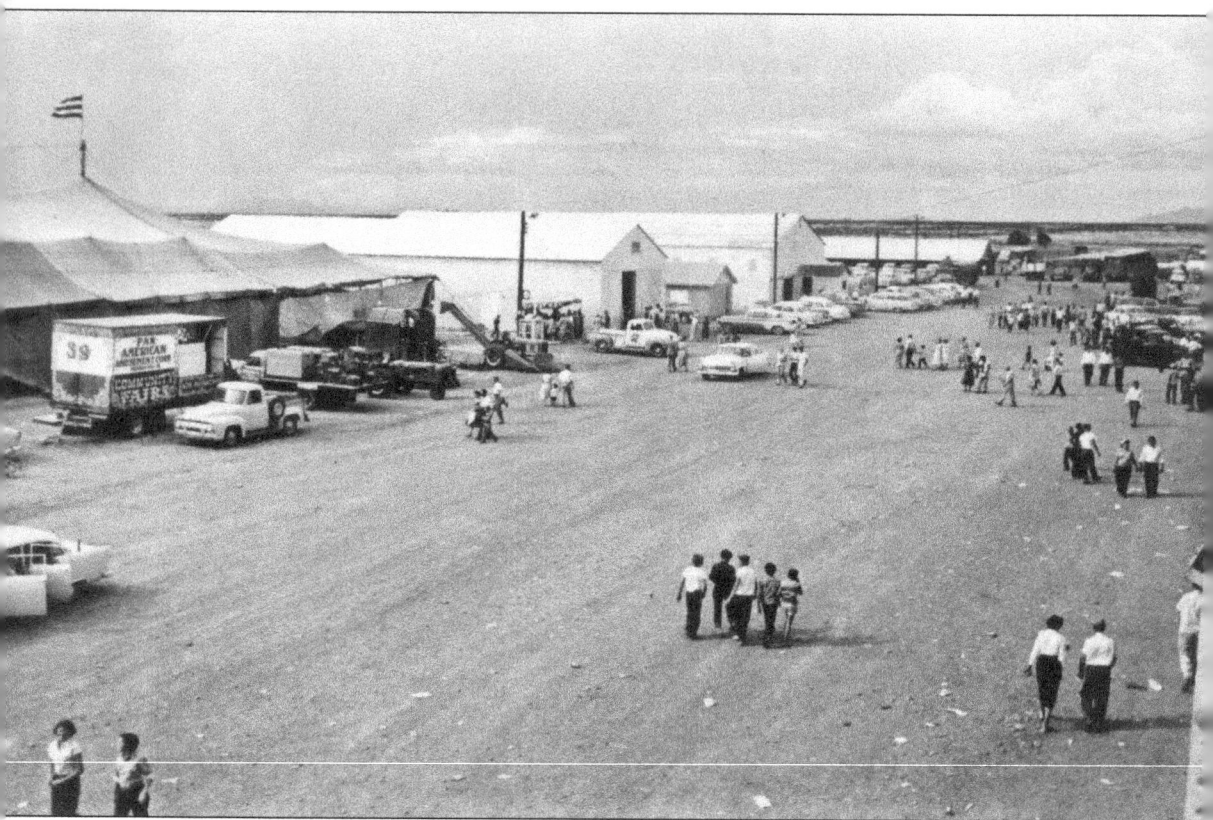

The first Cochise County Fair held in Douglas was from November 17 to 19, 1921. County fairs were held sporadically before that year at other locations, but the fair in Douglas had B. A. Packard as its chairman, and he established an association that still runs the fair today. In 1921, after a squadron of U.S. Army aircraft transferred to El Paso, the nascent fair association obtained use of the squadron's airfield and associated buildings for the first fair. Gradually the fair association board added buildings, and the fairgrounds appear today much as it does in this 1960s photograph. The beam on the right side of this photograph, taken from atop the grandstand, came from the dismantled Copper Queen smelter and, along with other girders from the smelter, constitutes the grandstand's underpinnings.

Eight

SPORTS

Sports have always been a part of Douglas's vitality. As early as 1903, the athletic members of the Thirteen Club held track-and-field meets during club picnics. They also formed Douglas's first baseball team.

In 1910, baseball fans raised $2,500 to build a 600-seat stadium. Sportsmen's Park featured a large canopy over the seats and a fenced ground large enough to accommodate baseball and football fields, east of San Antonio Avenue between Eighth and Ninth Streets.

"Those fields were full of stickers," recalled Joe Causey. He was a star back on the Douglas High School football team in 1925 and 1926. He went to the University of Alabama and played in a Rose Bowl before becoming a dentist and later Douglas mayor.

Another outstanding Bulldog football player was Gib Dawson. By the time he played, between 1946 and 1949, the football field was in front of a cement stadium, built just north of Fifteenth Street Park during the Great Depression. Dawson earned All-American honors at the University of Texas and played for the Green Bay Packers.

Dawson played several times for the Copper Pick, the trophy awarded to the winner of the Bisbee-Douglas game played on Thanksgiving Day. The series began in 1906, making it the oldest football rivalry in Arizona and one of the oldest prep rivalries in the country.

The passion generated by the Copper Pick game was matched by Douglas residents' love of baseball. In the 1950s, Douglas was home to the Copper Kings, a major-league farm team. The Copper Kings played in a stadium named for them, just east of the football field.

In 1958, while part of the Pittsburgh Pirates system, the Copper Kings set a record not likely to be equaled. In a game played against Chihuahua City, every King starter hit a home run. The feat won the game and helped the Kings win the Arizona-Mexico League season.

Douglas residents consistently support youth baseball, making Little League and Babe Ruth play a summer tradition. In 1965, Douglas hosted a regional Babe Ruth tournament and the next year the Babe Ruth World Series.

The first golf course in Arizona is believed to be this one in Douglas. This clubhouse at 1565 Twelfth Street and nine holes were created in 1907. The golf course stretched northwestward from the clubhouse, and tennis courts were west of the building. The Great Depression brought about the demise of this first golf club, but another took its place shortly after World War II. Local enthusiasts built the Douglas Country Club east of the fairgrounds, which expanded to 18 holes in the 1980s. Facilities include a swimming pool and RV park.

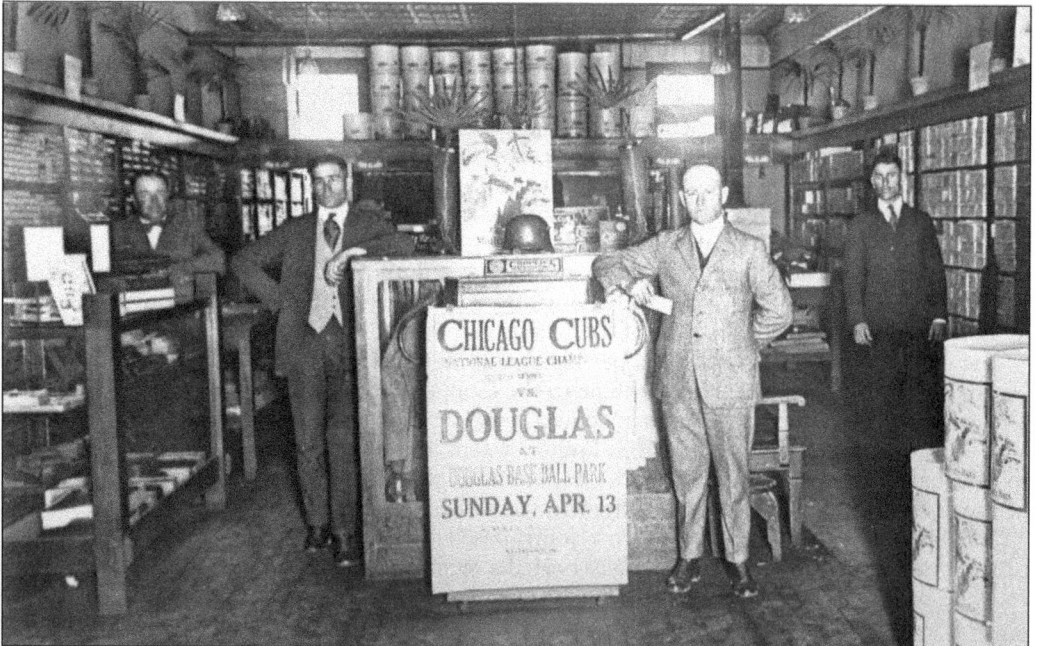

In the spring of 1919, the Chicago Cubs toured the country, playing local teams at every stop. On April 13, the National League champs were in Douglas to play a pickup squad. President of the Douglas Baseball Association, Charles R. Scott (second from left), sold tickets to the game in his men's clothing store, at 1029 G Avenue. Ticket costs ranged from 50¢ for children and 68¢ for soldiers, to $1.50 for a box seat. The Cubs won 14-3. (Courtesy Roy Manley.)

Sports were a popular pastime at Camp Harry J. Jones. Cavalry officers played polo against army teams from Fort Huachuca and Fort Bliss, Texas. Enlisted men played football (above) and baseball (below). The intense expression of the football coach leads one to believe he could be an excellent drill sergeant. (Both Courtesy Douglas Historical Society.)

In 1958, the Douglas Copper Kings, then part of the Pittsburg Pirate farm system, won the Arizona-Mexico League pennant and set a record enshrined in the Baseball Hall of Fame. In a game played on August 19 in Chihuahua City, each King starter hit a home run, whitewashing the Dorados 22-8. The nine starters were, from left to right, Fred Filipelli, Luis Torres, Darrell McCall, Ron Wilkins, player/manager Bob Clear, Andy Prevedello, Don Pulford, Dick Binford, and Dutch VanBurkleo.

During an assembly held November 29, 1962, at Douglas High School, Bisbee High School student body president John Sefferovich (left) handed over the Copper Pick trophy to Douglas High School student body president Frank Roqueni (right). The Bulldogs had defeated the Pumas 40-0 in the Thanksgiving Day game that renewed the oldest prep football rivalry in Arizona. Supervising the exchange are Bisbee coach Al Ridgeway and Douglas coach Charles Willingham. (Courtesy Frank Roqueni.)

From August 18 to 28, 1966, Douglas hosted the Babe Ruth World Series. Regional championship teams traveled to Douglas, as did Claire Ruth, widow of the Babe. She received gifts from Gadsden Hotel manager Henry Perez (white jacket), Agua Prieta city manager Crisoforo Romero, and Douglas mayor Joe Causey (behind Perez). Looking on is Ike Sharp (right), local organizer of the series. The New Orleans team (below) won the double-elimination tournament.

In 1954, the Douglas Elks Little League team won the Arizona championship and traveled to California for regional play. Members of that team included, from left to right, (first row) Bobby Page, Tommy Campbell, Ruben Rivas, Joe Scarpignato, Manuel Escarcega, Ruben Altamirano, and Richard Grajeda; (second row) coach Tom Campbell Sr., Fernando Roqueni, Ricardo Galindo, Roy Hernandez, Richard Ruterman, Edmond Lewis, Hector Aldana, Thomas Sanders, coach Jack Murray.

Cochise College teams have been part of the Douglas sports scene for about 40 years. Men's basketball coach Jerry Carrillo, shown here in game mode, imparts an intensity to his players that has produced an overall winning record, conference championships, and consistent ranking of the Apaches in the nation's top-10 academic, junior college teams. (Courtesy Bruce Whetten.)

Nine

CIVIC LIFE

Unlike the years following World War I, copper prices stayed up following World War II. This fueled an economic boom that made Douglas bustle. For example, six separate automotive dealerships sold Nash, DeSoto, Willys, Dodge, General Motors, and Ford vehicles in 1950s Douglas.

The most prominent evidence of Douglas's prosperity was construction of a new high school. Dedicated in 1949, the campus included a large gymnasium moved 50 miles to Douglas from Fort Huachuca.

World War II had brought military men from all over the country to Douglas. After the war, many returned. They sparked renewed interest in the tourism potential of Douglas–Agua Prieta and the surrounding area.

With this came a growing realization of how entwined Douglas and Agua Prieta had become. For instance, the 1948–1949 Douglas City Directory listed Agua Prieta businesses as well as those in Douglas.

Another reality of the time was the increasing power of smelter worker unions. Many members were Hispanic military veterans who had seen the world outside of Douglas and returned to their hometown determined to change prejudicial attitudes. Triennial strikes became a feature of Douglas life, as did increasing affluence for Hispanic families.

Douglas's prosperity continued into the 1960s. In 1967, Mayor Joe Causey dedicated a new city hall, across Tenth Street from the old facility. Moving into the new building from the old building was Percy Bowden, who was recognized as the longest-serving police chief in the country.

Another addition to Douglas in 1962–1964 was Cochise College, 8 miles west of town, built on land donated by Mr. and Mrs. E. J. Bergman. It was part of a statewide system that was the brainchild of part-time Douglas resident A. R. Spikes. As a state senator, he shepherded bills through the Arizona legislature creating junior colleges that have educated more than 10,000 people.

The new college, combined with the smelter and border trade, kept Douglas's economy robust through the 1970s, but that would change in the next decade.

Dr. J. J. P. Armstrong (upper left) served as a surgeon for the Constitutionalists during the 1915 Battle of Agua Prieta and went overseas with the Canadian Army during World War I. His photographs helped popularize the "Wonderland of Rocks" and turn it into Chiricahua National Monument in 1936. Ynacio Soto (above right) managed the International Commission, a customs brokerage connected to the Constitutionalists in 1917. In the 1940s, he was president of Sonora's Portland Cement franchise and elected Sonoran governor. Franklin O. Mackey (left) owned the Kentucky Distillery Company in Juarez, Chihuahua, when he purchased the Gadsden Hotel in 1926. After rebuilding the hotel following the 1928 fire (page 59), Mackey operated it until 1945 when he sold it and retired. (The two above photographs, author's collection.)

Pure Food Bakery, at 1116 G Avenue, was one of six bakeries in Douglas when it opened in 1916. Twenty years later, it was the only bakery in town. Its owner, Conrad Kaiser (right), kept its equipment modern, including this row of delivery trucks (above). Pure Food's mixing machine held 500 pounds of flour in one batch and the main oven's capacity was 700 loaves. The loaf-slicing machine in the front window always attracted an audience marveling at sliced white bread.

When these photographs were taken about 1950, Richard Washington (above, left) and Kendall Melcher (above, right), partners in the Douglas Hardware Company, stocked thousands of items in their store at 933 G Avenue. Washington's father, William, a descendant of George Washington's brother, founded the store in 1909. Melcher, who grew up in Nacozari and graduated from the University of Arizona, joined Washington in the late 1920s. Their store was north of an unofficial line dividing Douglas's downtown at that time; stores south of Ninth Street attracted mostly Mexican clientele, while those north of Ninth Street were patronized mainly by Anglos.

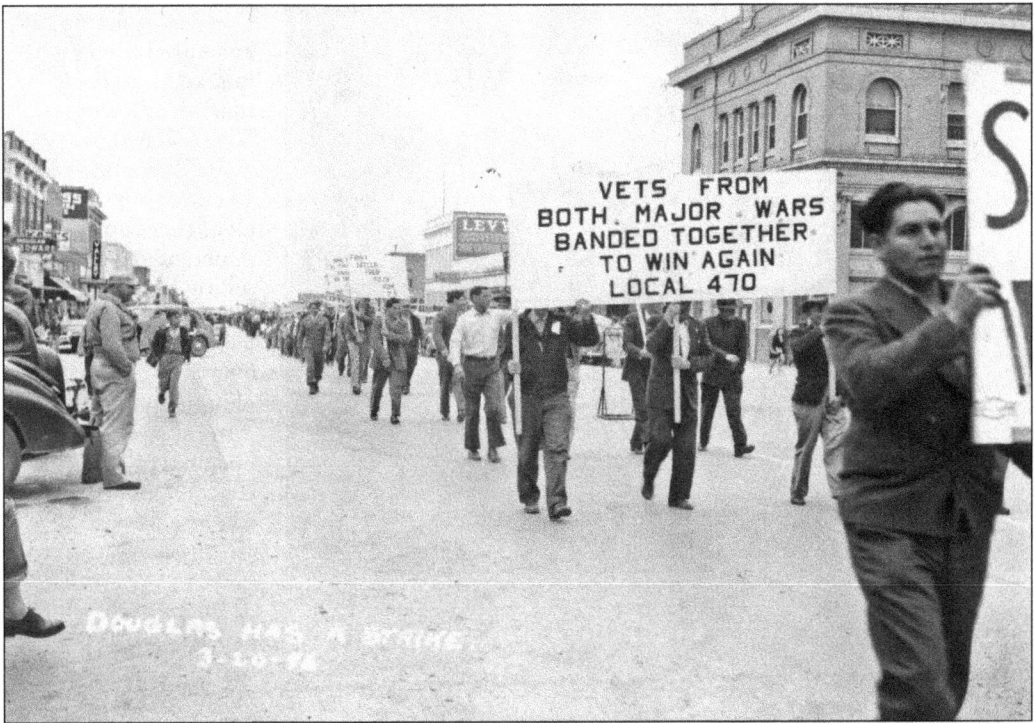

On March 20, 1946, members of CIO Local No. 470 marched up G Avenue as part of their strike against Phelps Dodge Corporation. Smelter worker unions gained power during the next 10 years by acquiring many members who were Hispanic veterans of World War II. The signs these strikers carry reflect their military service (notice some are in uniform) and the men's determination to gain higher wages so as to provide prosperity and dignity for themselves and their families. (Courtesy Douglas Historical Society.)

Douglas–Agua Prieta benefitted from a renewed interest in tourism following World War II. In 1949, Agua Prieta boasted 13 curio shops, almost all of them on Pan American Avenue, selling Mexican and imported goods to locals and tourists. The store in this photograph is La Azteca, owned and operated by Jose Castellanos and his son Jose Jr.

Two types of tourism are on display in this publicity photograph taken about 1948. The four people all have Mexican curios and are walking toward the station wagon that bears an "Em Bar Bee Guest Ranch" sign. They are, from left to right, Bud McCormick Jr., ranch manager; Barbara Reynolds, ranch guest; Mary McCormick, ranch owner; and Hermione (McCormick) King. Hermione was the wife of John M. "Dusty" King, a B-Western movie star in the 1930s and early 1940s. When this photograph was taken, King was the manager of KAWT, Douglas's first radio station, now known as KDAP. The Em Bar Bee, near Elfrida, is now a juvenile rehabilitation facility operated by Vision Quest.

In 1906, the kiosk in the above photograph was Douglas's first customshouse. The building in the top photograph on page 31 replaced the tiny 1906 structure. During 1932–1933, a new customs building, seen below, took shape at the Douglas Port of Entry. Although numerous modifications and additions were made in succeeding years, the outlines of the 1930s building are still visible today.

It took two years to build a new Douglas High School (above). On December 11, 1949, people gathered for a ceremony dedicating the gymnasium as Memorial Field House to honor Douglasites killed during World War II. On December 18, 1949, a ceremony, followed by a barbecue dinner, dedicated the high school itself (below). Among those attending were former Douglas mayor Everett J. Jones (seated, middle left) and seated clockwise (starting with Jones) are Phelps Dodge executives Mansell Visick, Robert Page, Cleveland Dodge, Walter Lawson, and Charles Kuzell.

Anna M. Dyer was the first female superintendent of Douglas Schools. She took on the job in September 1905 when the school district's first superintendent, Thomas Grindell, failed to return from a summer vacation exploration of Sonora; one person from the expedition showed up in a crazed condition, but Grindell's body was never found. Dyer served until January 1906.

William E. Lutz (upper left) was the third superintendent of Douglas Schools, holding the job until 1916. During his tenure, the district built 10 schools and enrollment grew by over 2,500 students. Ralph E. Souers (upper right) succeeded Lutz, but he resigned in 1918 to conduct civilian training during World War I. In the 1920s, Souers started a private boys school in the Chiricahua Mountains. Superintendent Hollis E. Stevenson (left) was known for his emphasis on building maintenance—an important matter during his 1948–1964 tenure when district enrollment jumped by 1,400 students. Douglas's newest primary school is named for him.

This aerial photograph of Douglas's church square, the 700 block bounded by Tenth and Eleventh Streets and D and E Avenues, was taken sometime between 1958 and 1965. First Presbyterian Church (bottom right corner) erected its education building (the large, white roof) in 1958. In 1965, St. Stephen's Episcopal (top right corner) connected its church and parish hall with a string of classrooms that do not appear in this photograph. The other churches on the square are Grace Methodist (top left) and First Baptist (bottom left).

Phelps Dodge Corporation constructed a hospital on the northeast corner of Ninth Street and F Avenue in 1939. The brick, cruciform building replaced the Calumet and Arizona Hospital, at 640 Tenth Street, and the Copper Queen dispensary, at 745 Ninth Street. After closing the hospital in the 1980s, Phelps Dodge donated the building to Douglas ARC, a non-profit corporation that assists the community's mentally handicapped residents with a variety of innovative programs under the direction of Gary Clark. (Courtesy Douglas Historical Society.)

Phelps Dodge Mercantile opened its store in Douglas in 1903 and closed it in 1988. That means the Douglas "PD Merc" may have been the oldest, continually operated, major retail store in Arizona. When this photograph was taken about 1963, the grocery, hardware, and drug departments, along with clothing and shoes, were on the ground floor. Furniture, appliances, and toys filled the second floor, meaning children keen on seeing the latest playthings had to climb three flights of stairs, past the offices in the mezzanine, before reaching the bliss of the toy department.

In 1966, someone climbed to the second floor of the old city hall and took this photograph of the new city hall under construction in the 400 block across Tenth Street. The Palomar Hotel (page 19), an office building, and the old armory were cleared to make way for the new municipal government building.

When Percy Bowden became Douglas police chief in 1920, he already had established his reputation by catching bootleggers as a Cochise County sheriff's deputy. Bowden was also famous as John Dillinger's jailer after the Chicago gangster's capture in Tucson in 1934. This photograph was taken about 1949. Bowden retired in 1971 after a 50-year career, making him the police chief who served the longest time of any in the country.

Horse-drawn fire engines used to leave on calls from Douglas City Hall. In 1912, Douglas was spread out enough that the fire department established a second fire station at 1400 Tenth Street. In the above photograph, fire chief Hugh Kelly stands with some of his men at the auxiliary station. In the photograph below, taken in 1985, the greatly modified station has William Hudspeth as chief. The man in light-colored pants is Douglas police chief Joe Borane.

Three Douglas mayors in the second half of the 20th century were Henry Beumler, Joe Causey, and Ben F. Williams Jr. All three grew up in Douglas, left for a period of time, and returned to their roots. Beumler (upper right) was the son of one of Douglas's first attorneys and judges. He too became an attorney and later taught at Douglas High School. Causey (upper left) was a star Bulldog athlete who played in a Rose Bowl game for the University of Alabama while on his way to becoming a dentist. As mayor, Causey oversaw construction of the new city hall building. Williams (right), an attorney, had the difficult job as mayor of seeing Douglas through its transition from smelter town into border town. (All courtesy City of Douglas.)

This horse's name is Relampago (Lightning) and he was as fast as his moniker. His owner, Agua Prieta nightclub owner Rafael Romero, looks justifiably pleased with his mount, since Relampago had won two match races that made him a celebrity. The first race occurred in 1957 on an Agua Prieta street. Relampago beat El Moro de Cumpas, a horse named for his Sonoran hometown. Leonardo Yañez, a Douglas resident, wrote a *corrido* (ballad) about the race that is still a standard tune in Mexico and was the inspiration for a motion picture. The second race, in 1958, found Relampago running on the Mexican side of the international border and defeating his opponent on the American side. Relampago became so famous his charity appearances built schools and hospitals, and Mexican president Luis Echevarria came to see him in 1970.

One of the nation's top-selling records in 1949 was "[Ghost] Riders in the Sky," written by Stan Jones, a Douglas native whose inspiration for the hit single was another Douglas man, Levi Watts. Jones grew up in Douglas and became friends with Watts, an old cowpoke who lived a primitive existence on Saddlegap Mountain east of town. Jones wrote many other songs, including the theme for the classic motion picture, *The Searchers*, and other John Ford Westerns. He also appeared in several Walt Disney feature films and starred in a television show, *Sheriff of Cochise County*, which was on the air in the late 1950s. Jones was inducted in to the Western Music Hall of Fame in 1997.

Corp. Robert Fred Hilburn
Co. L . 335 th. Infantry .—
Killed in action Sept. 18. 1918 at Benney, France.

By 1959, about when this photograph was taken, the Fred Hilburn American Legion Post Drum and Bugle Corps had won eight state championships between 1951 and 1958 with a prior string of eight wins between 1938 and 1949. The post was named for Cpl. Fred Hilburn (left), a veteran of the Punitive Expedition and member of Company L, 335th Infantry, who died in France on September 20, 1918, two days after receiving an abdominal wound during World War I. Drum and Bugle Corps members were, from left to right, (first row) Mike Shaya, David Cantua, ? Rivera, Mal Barrett, Mariano ?, Jessie James, Mike Cooney, unidentified, Greg Gomez, unidentified, and Bill Scott; (second row) George Birch, Frank Nobels, Wayne Stuart, Albert Johnson, George Warne, Charlie Sundt, unidentified, "Stubb" Evans, Roy Manley, unidentified, Jim Byerly, and unidentified; and (third row) unidentified, Frank Cantua, Sam Arciniega, Martin Chavez, Ray de la Torre, "Nacho" Vindiola, Quint Cabarga, and Reed Halverson.

The Douglas Art Association began as an informal group during the 1950s, and by the 1960s was a non-profit corporation that sponsored various events, including the annual Two Flags Festival of the Arts. Eight past presidents of the group gathered for this 1983 photograph. They were, from left to right, Jo Shaya, 1959–1960; Kitty Deiss, 1966–1968; Joyce Smith, 1968–1970 and 1978–1980; Norma Gerbich, 1976–1977; Bee Jay Zans, 1977–1978; Marge Mock, 1982–1984; Terry Mason, 1980–1982; and, in front, Jean Gertsch, 1972–1973. (Courtesy Douglas Art Association.)

Cochise County senator A. R. Spikes (left) was living in Douglas part-time when he and another Douglas resident, Charles Bloomquist, who was a state representative, wrote a bill creating Arizona's junior college system. The third college founded as a result of their bill was Cochise College (above). After Cochise County voters approved a $1.6 million bond issue for building construction, the first Cochise classes were held September 21, 1964, on a campus between Douglas and Bisbee. It included a student union, library, gym, and two residence halls. Today Cochise students prepare for university classes or pursue vocational degrees in nursing, aviation, or other fields.

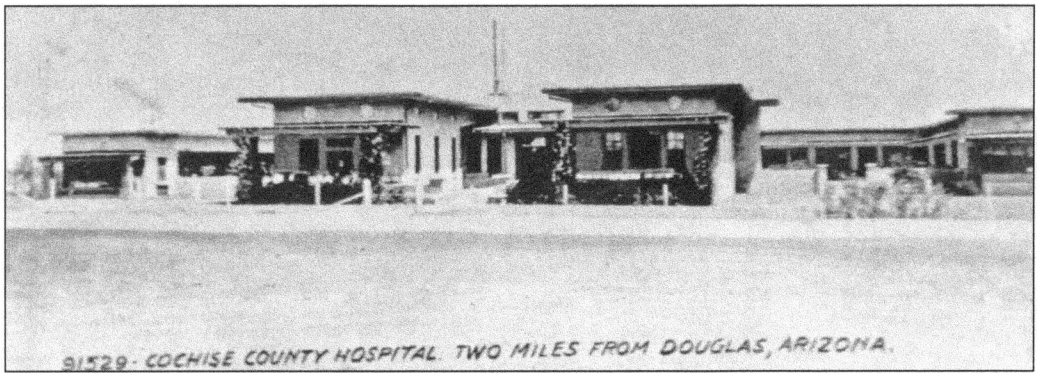
91529 - COCHISE COUNTY HOSPITAL. TWO MILES FROM DOUGLAS, ARIZONA.

Cochise County moved its hospital (top) to Douglas in 1910. The first superintendent was Dr. F. W. Randall, the man in the photograph at the top of page 17. By the 1970s, when the hospital was remodeled (middle), management companies provided health services to residents of Douglas and the surrounding area. After one of those companies went bankrupt in 1998, Dr. George Spikes (right) formed a non-profit corporation that put the hospital back on solid financial ground, where it is today.

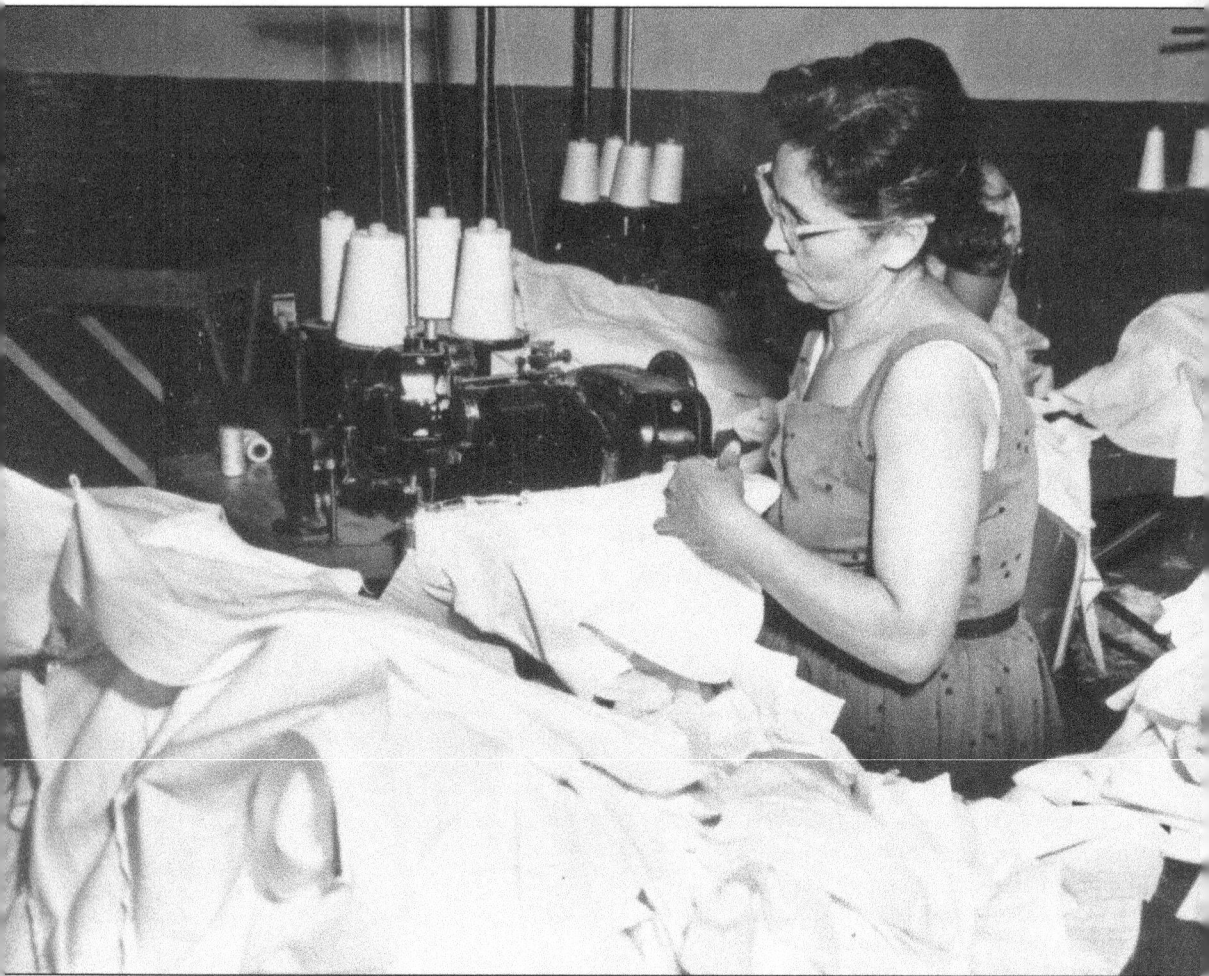

A success story among the efforts to diversify Douglas's manufacturing sector began about 1960. Delta Shirt Manufacturing Company opened a facility in Douglas where workers such as this one created clothing sold around the country. By 1969, ownership changes had Douglas's sewing factory owned by Woods Company, which initiated the first twin plant (a maquiladora) in the area. The twin-plant concept took advantage of tariff reductions by Mexican and American governments, which allow for flow of American parts into Mexico where assembly takes place. Manufactured items are returned to the United States for shipping.

Ten

POST SMELTER

Increasing environmental awareness in the 1960s and 1970s focused attention on Douglas's smelter, whose age made it almost impossible to retrofit pollution controls. Phelps Dodge negotiated with federal and state officials to prolong operations, but clearly the smelter's days were numbered.

Bisbee's open pit mine closed in 1976 and underground work ceased in 1978. The Douglas smelter became a custom operation, but even that stopped in 1987. Dismantling began in 1988, and the stack came down on January 13, 1990.

Anticipating smelter closure, Mayor Ben F. Williams Jr. encouraged construction of an Arizona State Prison Complex. Work began in 1983 on the first minimum-medium security unit at Bisbee-Douglas Airport. In 1984, the state converted a Douglas motel into a unit for DUI offenders.

Douglas merchants began relying on border trade. Despite peso devaluations, many northern Mexico residents shopped regularly in Douglas. In 1992, this prompted construction of a new shopping area, west of Pan American Avenue with Fifth Street as access.

The new area's anchor was the largest Safeway in Arizona. A Wal-Mart followed, but it adversely affected many downtown merchants, resulting in numerous empty buildings. The overall result of Wal-Mart's Douglas presence, however, was increased sales tax revenue.

Another contributor to the area economy are twin plants (maquiladoras), in which American-made parts assembled in Mexico are returned to the United States for shipping. Goods locally manufactured under this arrangement include seat belts, electronics, and clothing.

Some products flowing across the border are illegal. Drug smuggling, and associated activities such as money laundering, developed an underground economy in Douglas. How big a part they played became clear on May 17, 1992, when federal authorities raided a Douglas lumberyard and discovered a professionally engineered tunnel linking it with a house one block south in Agua Prieta.

In 2003, pursuit of human smugglers resulted in construction of the largest U.S. Border Patrol station in the country, 6 miles west of Douglas. Law enforcement agencies remained the town's largest employer until 2008 when Advanced Call Technologies, a call center firm, opened a facility in town. Plans call for employment of almost 700 people by 2010.

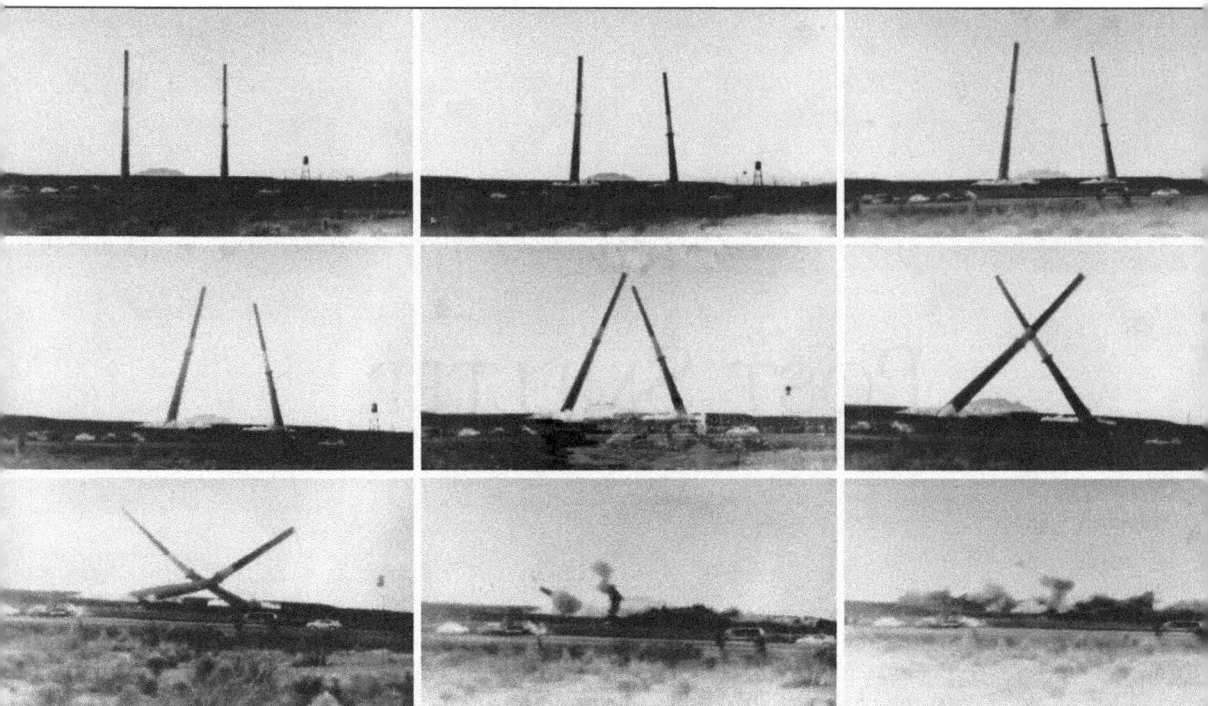

Going. . . . Going. . . . Gone! The Douglas Reduction Works cast its last anodes in 1987. Dismantling began two years later, and the stacks came down in 1990.

When this photograph was taken in 1991 at the Bendix Safety Systems factory in Agua Prieta, it and another Douglas twin plant produced 65 to 75 percent of all the seat belts manufactured in North America. The Bendix *maquila* was then manufacturing about 25,000 front and rear seat belts daily, but at full production it could turn out 40,000 each day.

When Douglas resident Bob Fernandez (above, right) talked with Congressman Jim Kolbe (above, left), Fernandez already had many years experience in the twin-plant sector. He put that experience to use by starting his own company that provides contracting and shelter options to firms considering *maquila* operation. In 1991, Fernandez's clients included United Engine Corporation, which manufactured replacement pistons for Chevrolet automotive engines (below).

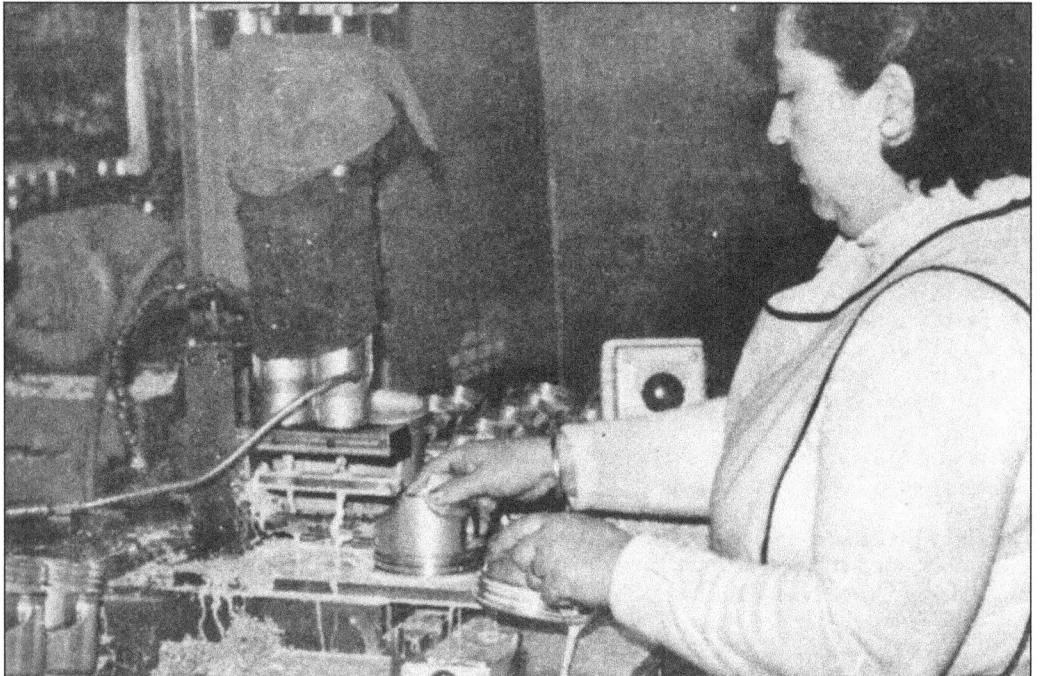

In 1991, the oldest twin plant in Douglas–Agua Prieta was White Knight Health Care, which manufactured disposable medical and industrial garments made of nonwoven, pulp-based fabric. This material was cut in Douglas by experienced workers, such as this one, sent to Agua Prieta and made into garments, and returned to Douglas before sterilization and shipping to hospitals, clinics, and laboratories around the United States.

A May 17, 1992, raid on a Douglas business revealed border trade of an illegitimate sort. Federal agents entered Douglas Building Supply, in the 600 block of First Street, and found a 200-foot-long, concrete-lined tunnel that connected the Building Supply lumber room with a house in Agua Prieta. Agents displayed a large amount of seized cocaine (left) that had been sent through the tunnel 30 feet underground and transported in specially constructed Building Supply trucks. The tunnel attracted much attention, which began to taper off when Mexican authorities sealed the tunnel's southern entrance with cement (below).

The U.S. Border Patrol first placed units in the Douglas area in the 1920s. Seventy-five years later, Douglas became the site of the largest Border Patrol station in the nation, at 53,000 square feet with a separate maintenance building. The station is 6 miles west of Douglas and was dedicated in March 2003. This station replaced one built in 1986 north of Douglas, which now hosts horses from mounted units, such as the ones in this photograph. (Author's collection.)

The first of five units in the Arizona State Prison Complex at Douglas became operational in December 1983. The fourth unit was a facility for DUI offenders placed in a converted Douglas motel during the spring of 1984. Many of the 2,150 inmates in the complex "give back" to the community by working on projects such as this installation of new flooring for the Douglas Art Association when it moved into the former Douglas Library in 2000. (Author's collection.)

A. J. Bayless Markets opened a store in Douglas on August 2, 1960. Over 450 automobiles jammed the parking lot, and hundreds of people shopped inside the 50,000-square-foot building. The parking lot and square footage of the building, which had been empty since the early 1990s, in 2008 attracted Advanced Call Center Technologies. The City of Douglas purchased the building and renovated it, using prison labor, so that Advanced Call Center could lease the building. The firm expects to have almost 700 Douglas employees by 2010.

BIBLIOGRAPHY

Arizona, The Youngest State. S. J. Clarke Publishing Company, 1916.

Cleland, Robert Glass. *A History of Phelps Dodge, 1834–1950.* New York: Alfred A. Knopf, Inc., 1952.

Jeffrey, Robert S. *The History of Douglas, Arizona.* Masters degree thesis written for the University of Arizona, 1951.

Myrick, David F. *Railroads of Arizona, Volume 1.* Berkeley, CA: Howell-North Books, 1975.

Nichols, Charles A. *Dear Old Cochise.* Unpublished manuscript in author's possession.

Reinhold, Ruth M. *Sky Pioneering.* Tucson, AZ: University of Arizona Press, 1982.

"Who's Who In Arizona." 1913. *Arizona Daily Star Press.*

Wiggans, Gladys Genevieve. "A History of the Douglas Public Schools, 1901–1965." Written for Douglas Schools Board of Education, 1965.

Visit us at
arcadiapublishing.com

www.ingramcontent.com/pod-product-compliance
Lightning Source LLC
Chambersburg PA
CBHW080620110426
42813CB00006B/1567